LEADERSHIP,
REINVENTED

LEADERSHIP, REINVENTED

How to Foster Empathy, Servitude, Diversity, and Innovation in the Workplace

Hamza Khan

ROCKRIDGE
PRESS

Interior and Cover Designer: Linda Snorina
Art Producer: Tom Hood
Editors: Marisa Hines and Samantha Holland
Production Editor: Emily Sheehan

Cover illustration © Gail Armstrong, 2020
Author photo courtesy of Abhav Sidhu

ISBN: Print 978-1-64611-955-4 | eBook 978-1-64611-956-1
R0

For Niki Strachan,
James Hunt, and the bright
young leaders of Newcastle,
New South Wales . . .
Thank you for the call to
adventure.

CONTENTS

INTRODUCTION

Welcome to *Leadership, Reinvented*. My name is Hamza Khan, and I consider it an honor to be entrusted with your precious time and open mind. As such, I've endeavored to distill my sprawling leadership experience into actionable insights and practical advice that is tailored to you, the modern leader. I'm a modern leader myself; I've spent over a decade working at the intersection of marketing, education, skills training, and professional development. I have a track record of leading and coaching high-performing and award-winning teams at both scrappy start-ups and behemoth organizations alike. Throughout my career, my approach to leadership has been guided by the same unwavering principle: people over everything.

In 2015, I delivered a polarizing TEDx talk titled "Stop Managing, Start Leading." On one hand, it inspired and validated my fellow modern leaders. On the other, it startled and even insulted our traditional counterparts. In my address, I advanced a new model for leading in the future of work—one rooted in trust, optimism, co-creation, collaboration, and decentralization. Drawing from my experiences creating and leading highly effective and successful teams, I shared several best practices for leading the next generation, such as promoting flexibility, creating a healthy culture, driving coaching and mentorship, and supporting remote working. To my surprise, these now commonplace ideas were met with resistance. In fact, the day after the talk, my boss summoned me to his office. He relayed that some of his executive colleagues were appalled by my laissez-faire leadership style, concerned that I was promoting a seditious and ineffective model that would undermine their established order. He even suggested that I apologize for my tirade against outdated management practices. I'm glad I didn't.

Five years later, our world has drastically changed. And my TEDx talk has resonated globally, amassing over a million views (and counting). It's confirmation that we're ready to move away from avoidant, aggressive, and authoritarian manifestations of leadership, toward something more transformational. Something that bucks economic self-interest and promotes more equitable and sustainable outcomes. Leadership has been long overdue for reinvention.

A quick survey of our shifting surroundings reveals as much: from Colin Kaepernick's kneeling in 2016 to Harvey Weinstein's arrest in 2018; from the long-awaited ruling in favor of LGBTQIA+ workplace protections to the inevitable George Floyd protests in 2020; the call for a sweeping reset can no longer be ignored. This book's focus on the values of servitude, innovation, diversity, and empathy (you'll see them collectively referred to as SIDE) is purposeful. Attention to these values has been sorely lacking in the models that produced the asymmetry that has been destabilizing our world until recently.

There's a lot in this book that will challenge your worldview, and the benefits might not be immediate or obvious. But I ask you to trust me and to keep an open mind. What I'm about to share with you is undeniable, and it may fundamentally change your attitudes and perspectives. We'll begin with a deep dive into modern leadership in part 1. Then in part 2, we'll explore in detail the bright SIDE values: servitude, innovation, diversity, and empathy. Each of the four values has its own chapter (out of acronym order, but more on that later), as well as six tried-and-tested exercises to drive reinvention. In the final section of this book, I'll walk you through the creation of a leadership road map. It's a simple yet nuanced model that will help you remain focused and sustain progress.

If your process of reading this book is anything like my process of writing it, then prepare for profound change. Prepare to reinvent yourself and your organization. Whether you're a recently promoted leader, on track to a promotion, or a leader keen on shifting your perspective, I hope this book will serve you well. And in doing so, I hope that it will empower you to serve others just as well.

PART 1

CHANGE IS IN THE AIR

"If the past had taught me anything, it was that . . . something unpredictable will always happen; bad news becomes an inevitability."

— BOB IGER
(Former CEO of The Walt
Disney Company)

CHAPTER 1

What Does It Mean to Be a "New" Leader?

On March 11, 2020, the World Health Organization officially designated the global outbreak of COVID-19 as a full-blown pandemic. Within 72 hours, nations across the globe followed suit by declaring states of emergency. Faced with the unprecedented spread of a deadly virus, world leaders made the drastic and difficult decision to shut down society itself. They began by severely restricting travel, then by closing nonessential businesses. With new cases and death tolls exponentially increasing despite their efforts, the leadership apparatus we entrusted with our safety and well-being did the unthinkable: They imposed quarantines, forcing us all to shelter in place. Indefinitely.

Every business, government, and social enterprise leader on the planet—novice and veteran alike—confronted an indisputable truth: They were either ready for this leadership moment presented by sudden adversity, or they were not.

Just a few months earlier, in November 2019, the second leg of a speaking tour in Australia brought me to the quaint harbor city of Newcastle, New South Wales. There I delivered a keynote address to an audience composed of mostly students, early talent, and young leaders. It was a brand-new talk, titled "HUMAN 9000: Navigating the Future of Work through Attunement, Resilience, and Creativity." I was thrilled to find that its core message—"change or be changed"—resonated strongly with this group. An idea that seemed to have stuck out to James Hunt, one of the organizers, was my description of our rapidly changing world as defined by four overlapping characteristics:

- **Volatility:** Refers to the speed and dynamism of change. The more volatile the environment, the faster and further conditions change.

- **Uncertainty:** Refers to the predictability of events, including how they'll unfold. The more uncertain the environment, the harder it is to forecast.

- **Complexity:** Refers to the multitude and interconnectedness of factors that need to be considered. The more complex the environment, the harder it is to analyze.

- **Ambiguity:** Refers to a lack of clarity and overall obscurity of reality. The more ambiguous the environment, the harder it is to decipher.

Aaron McEwan, vice president of research and advisory at Gartner Inc., had coined the acronym "VUCA" a few days earlier at a leadership coaching conference in Brisbane, Queensland, summing up my disorderly description of our chaotic, multifarious, and expeditiously evolving world. It's a concept that will recur throughout this book's exploration of leadership. Our world is indeed VUCA: volatile, uncertain, complex, and ambiguous.

Whether you're a recently promoted leader, on track to a promotion, or an experienced leader keen on shifting your perspective, you cannot afford to avoid facing the rapidly changing world around you. In the past, industry and paradigm shifts granted leaders a more considerable margin for error. But as you'll learn in this chapter and throughout this book, in today's world, failing to prepare for future leadership moments can prove to be disastrous. To bravely navigate the uncharted waters before us requires a radical departure from previous practices of leadership. And the journey must begin by seeing the outdated models for the optical illusions that they are.

In March 2020, during the initial days of the global pandemic, my father suffered a shocking health scare. I vividly recall him acting anxious and fidgety throughout dinner. With his business deemed nonessential and indefinitely shuttered, he reluctantly wrestled with a bleak, unanticipated vision of the family's future. Later that night, I awoke to the sound of a loud thud on the floor. I bolted to the kitchen, and what I saw next became indelibly seared into my memory. My father, Mustafa Khan, lay on the floor, his body shaking. My final coherent thought before my survival instinct took control was both unsettling yet strangely reassuring: *This is it.* I thought, *This is the moment. Now what?*

Fighting back tears, I silently repeated those words to myself as I waited in the car outside of the hospital. After six excruciating hours in the ER, my father hobbled out in good health and greater spirits. Doctors concluded that his fainting and seizure was due to unmanaged stress, fatigue, and anxiety brought on by the transitory tension of the pandemic. Ultimately, my dad recovered, and his life has since returned to a "new normal." But it hasn't for me. Not by a long shot.

That brush with mortality opened up a portal into a "new abnormal"—a shifting reality where death is imminent and change is inevitable. I'm now always anticipating and preparing for the passing of my father. But this is neither a grim nor overbearing realization; rather, it's a realistic, optimistic, and even liberating one. Facing the future with eyes wide open, I've been given a chance to truly value the limited time that I have with my old man and to better position myself to react and adapt when his time comes. Whenever that is, I'll need to rely on my ability to stand out and move forward into whatever paradigm is on the other side of the leadership moment. In the meantime, preparation requires both deep insight and vast foresight.

A few days after my father emerged from the emergency room, Naval Ravikant—the co-founder and former CEO of the start-up platform website AngelList—tweeted the words that ultimately served as the impetus for me to explore modern leadership in the future of work. He wrote: "Leadership in the coming months, at every level, is the audition to lead in the coming years." His words crystallized a jumble of three intertwining ideas that I had been ruminating on over the past decade:

- Leadership is a values-based system of action. It requires operationalizing and maximizing a shared set of integrated positive values.

- New leadership requires a profoundly human touch. This involves leaning into attributes and behaviors like empathy and servitude that are traditionally overlooked as counterproductive.

- Change must happen long before change is required. Intentional self-disruption (or reinvention) is mandatory to survive and thrive in our VUCA world.

Any opportunity to influence an organization's renewal or decline is a *leadership moment*. In today's VUCA world, leadership moments come in higher volumes and at higher frequencies than ever before. For new leaders, this level of adversity can be exhilarating as well as debilitating.

Whether we're talking about the second industrial revolution or Blockbuster's bankruptcy in 2010; the global economic collapse of 2008 or game seven of the 2019 NBA Eastern Conference Semifinals; Harvey Weinstein's eventual sentencing in 2020 or Steve Jobs's untimely passing in 2011 . . . leaders were either prepared for those moments or they weren't. And the leadership they displayed during those junctures were incredibly important auditions for them to keep leading—or be replaced.

Like most, I used to believe in the conventional wisdom that leaders, when faced with difficulty and uncertainty, step up. That they somehow rise to the occasion. But I now know that this is nothing but an optical illusion—one caused by other leaders falling back, enabling successful leaders to stand out.

The reality is, leaders don't step up when faced with a leadership moment. They don't suddenly become better leaders because of an encounter with adversity or uncertainty—least of all during a crisis. After all, how could they? That's not how the human brain works. Contending with a sudden, stressful situation, the part of the brain known as the *amygdala* (responsible for perceiving emotions such as fear, as well as controlling aggression) hijacks control of our response to a stressor. This phenomenon is termed "amygdala hijack" by Daniel Goleman in his book *Emotional Intelligence*. It disables the part of the brain required for cognitive processes such as decision-making and overrides it with simple survival-driven options: fight, flight, or freeze.

Like any of us, when a challenging and unforeseen circumstance presents itself, a leader cannot fully control their reaction. In the words of heavyweight-champion-turned-philosopher Mike Tyson, "Everybody has a plan until they get punched in the mouth." Confronted by a moment of unexpected adversity, instinct almost always overrides rational thinking, and we fall back to the level of training and character that we've already established within ourselves.

If you're caught up in old paradigms, in a leadership moment you may default to decisions that will catalyze the destruction of your organization. But embracing new standards—especially the values of *servitude, innovation, diversity*, and *empathy*, SIDE (for short)—will allow you to anticipate and prepare for a leadership moment long before it happens, and we'll be exploring them deeply in the coming chapters of this book. You'll start by learning about the value of being able to empathize with others, and then build on that by understanding the value of leading through servitude, the importance of diversity and inclusion, and how innovation can help your organization succeed in the future. Embracing all these bright SIDE values will grant you resilience. And as a more resilient leader, you will create a more resilient organization. Together, you'll make the right decisions in the moments that will carry you forward.

We saw countless examples of this during the time of danger introduced by COVID-19 in 2020, which brought our world's VUCA characteristics into sharp focus. The pressure prompted many leaders to misstep, stumble, and collapse. Some fell back; others fell down. With every decision and reaction scrutinized, some titular leaders found themselves exposed as nothing more than glorified managers. Almost overnight, organizations of all shapes and sizes capsized; behemoth companies, which once appeared invulnerable, were suddenly hemorrhaging money and people.

How then, amid chaos, did some leaders seem so well prepared for the leadership moment? Why did some leaders effectively navigate the crisis, and why did others fail? The answer has nothing to do with "stepping up" and everything to do with the days, weeks, months, and years leading up to the leadership moment presented by the crisis. For the human-centric, change-friendly, self-disrupting, and values-driven modern leader, a crisis can be a moment of opportunity.

Leaders who stand out are prepared for adversity long before they know when and how adversity will present itself. The truth is, leaders don't even have to know the specifics about what challenges are coming—they simply need to remain vigilant and prepared for the unfamiliar. Modern leaders know that one day they will have to make tough decisions in response to factors outside of their control. And when that happens, they will default to the underlying, subconscious system that forms the basis of their decision-making during times of relative peace. And for them to rely on that system to produce good decisions, they have to train it like a muscle—every single day.

In other words, leadership is intentional. It's not something that just emerges when a crisis happens. Leadership is honed, operationalized, and maximized through daily decisions and imperative actions. Leadership is an ongoing practice—a way of thinking, being, and doing. It's an evolving, holistic exercise that prepares people to stand out (not step up) during critical moments. Leaders must plan for change long in advance. At the same time, they must be prepared to adjust the plan if necessary. Leadership, in this way, is the art of continuous reinvention.

In the coming chapters, and with the help of some familiar examples, you'll gain a deeper understanding of what it means to be a modern leader. Let's begin by exploring how you, as a new or reinvented leader, can positively impact an organization.

The Positive Impact New Leaders Can Have

Jack Welch, the former chairman and CEO of General Electric, is responsible for my go-to quote about organizational transformation: "If the rate of change on the outside exceeds the rate of change on the inside, the end is near." Welch's words succinctly capture the need for leaders to continually disrupt themselves (and by extension, their organizations).

Self-disruption—that inside change Welch refers to—is critical to the renewal of the organization. And renewal, an organization's partial or complete reinvention, is the antidote to collapse. It's essential to an organization's ability to succeed and journey across the chasm of time. Our increasingly VUCA world (volatile, uncertain, complex, and ambiguous; see page 4) has made it difficult for leaders to create traditional top-down, self-serving organizations, because those models don't support the pace of change that today's world requires. People around the world are demanding a newer and better type of company: one that creates value at all levels—for employees, customers, the environment, and society at large. This practice, achieved through the SIDE values (page 7), enables adaptability and empowerment in the face of change.

Leaders who are stuck in old ways of thinking are merely avoiding the reality of their predicament. They seem to have forgotten that all organizations are beholden to a typical life cycle:

1. **Introduction:** An organization is born and experiences an immediate surge in attention and success.

2. **Growth:** As the organization finds its place in the external environment, it surges and evolves.

3. **Maturity:** Once it achieves a sort of equilibrium within the landscape, its growth tapers off.

4. **Renewal or decline:** The trajectory of the organization always approaches an inflection point—one where it must renew the cycle or die.

This process looks different for every organization. It could be long and drawn out, like the demise of Kodak in 2012; it could be relatively instantaneous, like the bankruptcy of the XFL in 2020; or it could be lopsided, like the slow rise and rapid fall of WeWork in 2019. In all cases, failure to self-disrupt directly correlates with an organization's complete failure. No institution, regardless of how big or successful, is immune to this. Littering the seabed of history are the empty hulls of corporate, government, and social enterprises that didn't plan to change *as* necessary or change the plan *when* necessary.

But this is an avoidable fate. Enter the modern leader, who can introduce the sort of thinking and perspective necessary to disrupt and renew an organization *before* circumstances demand it. When duly empowered, these leaders can help an organization anticipate change and then adequately respond—often well in advance of when the change is actually required. Best of all, these leaders can easily replicate their leadership, creating more leaders to continue their organization's evolution long after they're gone. It all springs from SIDE: Exercising servitude, modern leaders optimize their team's productivity. Sparking innovation, they produce a future-focused culture. Driving diversity, they harness the full potential of their workforce. And practicing empathy, they develop true attunement with their environment.

What does such an organization look like? We can describe it this way:

- **Human-centric.** New leaders unlock the full potential of the varied perspectives, backgrounds, and experiences of their increasingly diverse workforce.

- **Change-friendly.** New leaders promote adaptation and resilience.

- **Self-disrupting.** New leaders adequately prepare their organization for the world that will be.

- **Values-driven.** New leaders galvanize support from a public demanding more equitable and sustainable outcomes for the world at large.

To illustrate the impact of this type of leadership even further, let's consider some modern, real-world examples. As each leader approached the inflection point at which their respective organizations would have to either renew or decline, these individuals instinctively knew what to do. Why? Because as leaders who are both self- and situationally aware, they had prepared for their leadership moment long before it happened.

CORPORATE EXAMPLE:

Eric Yuan, FOUNDER AND CEO OF ZOOM VIDEO COMMUNICATIONS

As the 2020 coronavirus pandemic took hold, it quickly became clear that Zoom Video Communications was in a pivot that would shape the company forever. To its founder and CEO Eric Yuan's surprise, Zoom's product was morphing from a profitable teleconferencing platform into a must-have social and educational tool, and at breakneck speed.

Yuan had built a wildly successful business. The $35 billion company boasted marquee clients such as Uber, Delta, Slack, Rakuten, Logitech, and Ticketmaster. And then, all of the sudden, the world needed Zoom to be something else.

One of Yuan's first acts as a reinvented leader in the throes of a global crisis was to offer his platform free to educators. He didn't have to do this, considering the massive opportunity cost. But he went ahead anyway, because it was the right thing to do. Such generosity was nothing new for Yuan, who'd been known to give nonprofits and other institutions in need free access to Zoom ever since he co-founded the business in 2011. Back then, he'd left an executive role at Cisco Systems, where he lost sleep after speaking with unhappy Webex customers. Realizing that dissatisfied customers are symptomatic of systemic failure, Yuan concluded that the only way to truly solve unhappy customers' problems was to reinvent the video conferencing solution from the inside out. And, more importantly, to cultivate goodwill along the way.

Fast-forward to the tumultuous transition from corporate video conferencing solution to a renewed business: Zoom suddenly stumbled. Several of the software's security flaws were exposed by journalists, earning the company a barrage of negative media coverage that undermined user trust. In the hands of a change-resistant leader, this scenario could have permanently eroded company value, or even tanked the company altogether. But not for Yuan. Rather than passing the buck, the change-friendly CEO took ownership: "We recognize that we have fallen short of the community's—and our own—privacy and security expectations," Yuan wrote in a blog post. "For that, I am deeply sorry."

It's important to note here that without an apology, little might have changed, as Zoom had already cornered the video conferencing market. The platform surpassed 200 million daily meeting participants in March 2020, taking nearly 50 percent of the total market share. But Yuan apologized anyway: "We did not design the product with the foresight that, in a matter of weeks, every person in the world would suddenly be working, studying, and socializing from home."

What allowed Yuan to respond so swiftly and effectively in that moment of crisis was not something he spontaneously conjured up at the moment. Quite the opposite—he defaulted back to a well-established value, one that he exemplifies as a person and that Zoom had operationalized and maximized: empathy.

In a 2017 interview, Yuan spoke candidly about Zoom's core principles, saying, "We expect our employees to care about the community, the company, their teammates, customers, and themselves. We don't want our Caring philosophy to be a one-off that is explained in employee training and then never discussed again, so it is posted on the wall of Zoom's lobby in every location, it is a common refrain in our all-hands meetings, and it is the core of the work at Zoom."

When Zoom was caught off guard by their sudden surge and stumble, all Yuan and his team had to do was default back to one of their values—the same one that enabled them to disrupt the market in the first place.

GOVERNMENT EXAMPLE:
Jacinda Ardern, PRIME MINISTER OF NEW ZEALAND

At 37, Jacinda Ardern became the second woman, and the youngest person, to ever lead New Zealand's Labor Party. In April of 2020, *The Atlantic* published an article titled "New Zealand's Prime Minister

May Be the Most Effective Leader on the Planet," about how Ardern's humanistic leadership style was resonating with people around the world. It was one of hundreds of articles about her showcasing to the world what leadership can look like in the face of adversity.

In just the first three years of her tenure, Ardern encountered a slew of leadership moments—including a handful that seriously tested her resolve and preparedness. And she met every single one of them swiftly and effectively. How? By being prepared well in advance.

Consider her reaction to the tragic Christchurch mosque shootings of March 2019. It's nothing short of a master class in transformational, human-centric leadership. For starters, Ardern communicated immediately, giving New Zealanders as much information as she could. Speaking clearly, she offered them the language required to unpack the unspeakable act, to vocalize the shock and sadness.

"They are us," she said of the dead and wounded. She added that New Zealand had been chosen for the heinous attack because it was safe, no place for hatred or racism: "Because we represent diversity, kindness, compassion. Home for those who share our values. Refuge for those who need it." She held steadfastly to those values and condemned the shooter.

Overnight, Ardern banned military-style semi-automatics and led the call for the removal of terrorist material online—two decisions which, by contrast, many world governments who experience more frequent terrorist attacks have routinely failed to make.

Focused on substantive change across the board, Ardern's vision for the future spans decades, if not centuries. When speaking about climate change at the 2019 World Economic Forum, for instance, Ardern posed the question, "Do you want to be a leader that looks back in time and say that you were on the wrong side of the argument when the world was crying out for a solution?" This rhetorical query reveals Ardern's hardwired predisposition to change:

" . . . that looks back in time" reveals her awareness of the nature of change.

" . . . the wrong side of the argument" reveals her understanding of the inflection point.

" . . . when the world was crying" reveals her attunement with broader contexts.

If her skillful handling of terrorism, a pandemic, and every other sudden challenge is emblematic of who she is as a human being, then Jacinda Ardern need not worry about being a leader on the wrong side of the argument, whatever the next challenge may be.

SOCIAL EXAMPLE:
Abel Tesfaye, La Mar Taylor, and Ahmed Ismail,
CO-FOUNDERS OF HXOUSE

The massive HXOUSE facility, located along Toronto's Waterfront, is a state-of-the-art multipurpose space, teeming with youth and early talent from every walk of life. Equal parts creative studio, training facility, start-up incubator, and co-working space, HXOUSE is something my friends and I, aspiring music video producers who shelved those dreams due to lack of resources, greatly needed when we were younger.

As it turns out, just a few blocks from where we grew up in Scarborough, Ontario, three promising young creators—Abel Tesfaye, La Mar Taylor, and Ahmed Ismail—persisted through similar challenges. Tesfaye would go on to become none other than megastar recording artist The Weeknd. Taylor became their record label's creative director. And Ismail grew into a force of nature in the world of PR. Having all achieved wild success in their respective endeavors, the three decided to pay it forward.

Thus was born HXOUSE, a not-for-profit organization dedicated to creating pathways into the entertainment industry for members of society with demonstrated need. Their mission is simple: Empower young entrepreneurs. As modern leaders, Tesfaye, Taylor, and Ismail knew that they would have to assemble the right team and curate the right partners to realize their bold vision of reducing barriers to access. Today, they lead a diverse collective of creatives and educators who activate the dynamic HXOUSE space. And they partner with the city of Toronto, major brands like Nike and Adidas, as well as accredited educational institutions to support future leaders.

Every HXOUSE graduate leaves equipped with the knowledge, experience, and exposure to become a leader in their own right. As leaders who practice servitude, the founding trio works tirelessly to support the next generation. One of their most recent projects, Black HXOUSE, empowers young female entrepreneurs of color to build their enterprises and navigate the tumultuous entertainment industry. It's an immersive program that includes high-profile mentorship and networking in addition to top-tier education. And it's just one of the many ways that HXOUSE is disrupting the traditional education system—the same one that failed to nurture the sparks of Tesfaye, Taylor, and Ismail.

In an interview with *Toronto Life*, Ismail shared that HXOUSE regularly makes him and his co-founders emotional. They often look at each other and say, "Man, I wish we'd had this."

Renowned business author Tom Peters once wrote, "Leaders don't create followers, they create more leaders." Leadership success is often a lagging indicator, appearing long after a leader's work is done. The three co-founders of HXOUSE believe that true success means their work will enable more diverse creatives to overcome obstacles, realize their dreams, and then pay it forward to the next generation.

True Leadership Creates More Leaders

All leaders are flawed. You are a flawed leader; I am a flawed leader. Yet, our failings don't make us failures. Quite the opposite: Leadership can be a messy undertaking that requires continually breaking down and building up again. The effective leaders spotlighted in this book possess qualities that allow them to innovate consistently, create value, and cross the chasm of time as individuals and as leaders of organizations. But, naturally, they are bound to make mistakes along the way. Perfection isn't their objective. Instead, they're trying to set up their respective entities—like Zoom, New Zealand, or HXOUSE—to learn from their mistakes and be victorious long after they're gone.

In effect, these leaders are almost writing themselves out of their roles by creating strong cultures and new leaders to carry their work forward. If done correctly, they will successfully replicate their leadership by codifying it in a road map, and by creating and empowering other leaders. In this way, a modern leader's work is always unfinished. While empowering more leaders might seem like giving away power that will lead to your own obsolescence, the opposite is true. The best leaders know that by empowering their team, they enable their organization to wholly renew itself time and again.

The Definition of a "New" Leader

The meaning of leadership has always been somewhat flexible. In the book *Leadership: Global and Regional Perspectives*, James Hunt breaks down the Old English etymology of "leadership," tracing its origins back to a pair of somewhat distinct meanings:

1. A person who guides, conducts, or shows the way—an individual with specialized or expert knowledge.

2. A ruler or chieftain, someone with widely recognized status and acknowledged authority over others.

Since about the year 2000, there has been an increasing tendency to add to those characterizations and redefine leadership as that which elicits voluntary followership. And even more recently, leadership has been repositioned as a system of action that is more humanistic, less exploitative, and more values-based.

The definition of a "new" or "modern" leader will continue to evolve, because change is part of the job description. New leaders respond successfully to leadership moments because they've been changing themselves, and their organizations, faster than the rate of change in their outside environment.

However the meaning of "leadership" is updated, we can certainly conclude that it won't encompass any of the leadership attributes from paradigms past. Modern leaders are not autocratic, transactional, directive, authoritative, bureaucratic, procedural, achievement-oriented, dictatorial, narcissistic, or exploitative. And the leaders who insist on clinging to those old ways are doomed to fail.

Consider Jack Dorsey and Elizabeth Holmes, polar opposites in terms of leadership styles. Dorsey, the co-founder and CEO of Twitter as well as the founder and CEO of Square, personifies the transformational leadership style advocated in this book. In a 2012 spotlight by *Forbes*, Dorsey said that the key to the success of Square is "transparency and trust." He insists that everyone who works for him knows what the company is up to and why, so much so that he instituted an astonishing rule at Square: At every meeting involving more than two people, someone must take notes—and send them to the entire staff. In response to a massive hack of high-profile accounts in 2020, Dorsey pledged even further transparency. He event went as far as detailing in a series of tweets precisely how the company will make things right.

Contrast Dorsey's hyper-transparency with Holmes's closed, secretive, autocratic leadership style. As detailed in *The Dropout* podcast, over the span of three years, an ABC News correspondent dove deeper into the investigations led by John Carreyrou of the *Wall Street Journal*, and examined the damning details behind the rise and fall of Holmes and her health tech company Theranos. Employees from the start-up disclosed that Holmes purposefully organized the company so that everyone was siloed. Employees weren't allowed to communicate with one another about their tasks, or their work in general. Consider that they also were advised not to reveal the company name on social media sites such as LinkedIn. One employee said that Holmes's style "went beyond micromanaging," adding, "it was a complete distrust for the organization that she'd built under her."

While Dorsey's Twitter and Square are thriving, Holmes's Theranos is now defunct. Two young Silicon Valley founders and CEOs, leaders of billion-dollar companies . . . why, reaching the same inflection point in their respective organizations' life cycles, did they go in such divergent directions? The answer goes back to ex–General Electric CEO Jack Welch's quote about change (page 9). Dorsey, unlike Holmes, embraced change early. He adopted a change-friendly mindset that allowed him to hit the reset button at multiple inflection points.

Though the impetus for change might come from outside the organization, the drive to change must come from within the organization. And it must be championed by a human-centric, change-friendly, self-disrupting, and values-driven leader who serves as the nucleus of the organization. This is the essence of a "new" (or reinvented) leader, whether it's someone who's literally new to the role or someone further along in their career who chooses to modernize their approach.

Let's examine this type of leadership by considering some famous modern leaders who were the first in their roles to be prepared for difficult leadership moments, enabling them to steer their organizations to success.

NEW LEADER EXAMPLE:
Indra Nooyi, CEO OF PEPSICO

As the recently appointed CEO of PepsiCo, Indra Nooyi would visit unsuspecting retail stores every week. There she would see how PepsiCo products appeared on shelves. She would take pictures of the products' packaging and placement and send feedback to the design and marketing teams. This is a practice that Nooyi—who was regularly named as one of the 100 most powerful women in the world by *Forbes*—would repeat for several of her first years in her new role. During a *Freakonomics Radio* podcast interview, she explained, "I look at our business through a different lens, and then I come back and I talk to my people about what I saw was good, and what wasn't really good."

Throughout her tenure as CEO, Nooyi transformed PepsiCo into one of the most successful food and beverage companies in the world. Her push for healthier snack and beverage choices, along with an eye for product packaging, drove an 80 percent sales growth in the 12 years she was CEO. Among her many achievements, she also helped PepsiCo make one of the biggest food deals in corporate history when they acquired Quaker Oats (which owned sports-drink brand Gatorade) for $13.4 billion.

The key to her success? Nooyi never stopped being a new leader: "I'm not just a CEO," Nooyi added during the same podcast episode. "I'm also a consumer." It was this level of harmony with the external environment—keeping her sensitive to its changes—that helped Nooyi navigate her way to the top of the company.

But perhaps the biggest mark of Nooyi's legacy was preparing PepsiCo in anticipation of the world that would come. In 2007 she hired PepsiCo's first chief scientific officer, Mehmood Khan, and its first director of global health policy, Derek Yach. "She was the first person to truly acknowledge that companies needed to change," Yach said. "She understood that very deeply, and started putting into place a couple of key elements that all companies now accept as normal."

While competitor companies were experimenting with new flavors, PepsiCo was tinkering with recipes that were lower in salt and fat, as well as recipes with non-sugar sweeteners. At the time, critics could reasonably point to Nooyi's investments and initiatives as shortsighted. Trendy diets were all the rage, but few had any staying power. But Nooyi, a forward-thinking modern leader, knew that their vision was limited: "The challenge of a leader," Nooyi said, "is looking around the corner and making the change before it's too late to make the change."

Today, years after Nooyi's bold moves, PepsiCo remains relevant among healthier consumers with a growing offering of organic, natural, and nutritious products. The shift was not a fluke. Nooyi—one of the 4.8 percent of Fortune 500 CEOs who are female, and one of the 13 percent who hail from outside the country where their firm's headquarters is located—has a long track record of seeing change long before it happens.

Follow Indra Nooyi's lead: Know that change must happen long before change is required. Lead a campaign to reinvent your organization from the inside out, for it's better to self-disrupt than to be disrupted.

NEW LEADER EXAMPLE:
Justin Trudeau, PRIME MINISTER OF CANADA

The social media class that I teach at Ryerson University always begins with students sharing current events. During a certain class in September 2019, everyone bought up the same item: Justin Trudeau's brownface scandal. If you're unfamiliar with this, brace yourself: It was revealed that the Canadian prime minister (who is white) wore heavy brownface makeup to a party at the private school where he was teaching at in 2001. Several photos had leaked from the party, adding more fuel to the fire.

Trudeau's political opponents were quick to call for his resignation. But Trudeau quickly apologized, saying: "I take responsibility for my decision to do that. I shouldn't have done it. I should have known better. It was something that I didn't think was racist at the time, but now I recognize it was something racist to do. And I am deeply sorry."

Even though he said all the right things, I personally still wasn't buying it. As a person of South Asian descent, Trudeau's use of the makeup struck me as more than indulgent—even suggestive of malice in his intent. My confidence in the leader had been shaken, as the photos suggested a distance between what Trudeau said and did publicly, and what he believed.

While he was running for office in 2015, though young and tagged by rivals as "just not ready" to be prime minister, Trudeau somehow seemed prepared for the future of our world. He demonstrated high emotional intelligence and spoke with compassion for vulnerable members of society. Trudeau painted a vision for what Canada, and the world, could be. Time and again, Trudeau stood out from the crowd. He admitted his mistakes, he gracefully responded to criticism, and he centered conversations around the needs of Canadian citizens. His vulnerable, human-centric approach to politics was a far cry from what Canadians were seeing in the world, and not just on the debate stage.

Since his reelection, Trudeau has continued to reinvent himself as a leader, speaking to—and working on behalf of—all Canadians more than ever before. And despite the speed bumps, Trudeau remained unwaveringly focused on creating a country that works for all Canadians. While his focus was fixed on his vision for the country, his approach has changed over time as needed. During intense moments when leadership was continuously tested, be they political scandals or pandemics, Trudeau didn't step up—he stood out. The leader Canada had during the quarantine was the person who was elected in the first place: a man who, despite his past and present follies, unwaveringly cares deeply enough about his people to allocate hard resources for students, charities, neglected territories, vulnerable populations, and those being left behind.

Follow Justin Trudeau's lead: Know that new leadership requires a profoundly human touch. There is true strength in seemingly counterproductive attributes and behaviors such as grace, humility, and compassion.

NEW LEADER EXAMPLE:
Tim Cook, CEO of Apple

I was initially puzzled by one of the first things that Tim Cook said, following his official installation as CEO in the wake of Apple founder and CEO Steve Jobs's untimely and shocking decision to step down. In an internal email to the company, Cook wrote: "I want you to be confident that Apple is not going to change."

Why would Cook say something that seems to go against Apple's core philosophy? Under Jobs's leadership, the company made products that changed computing as we know it. And now, here was Cook, his successor, saying that Apple was *not* going to change.

But all I had to do was read Cook's next few sentences to understand the game plan: "I cherish and celebrate Apple's unique principles and values. Steve built a company and culture that is unlike any other in the world and we are going to stay true to that—it is in our DNA. We are going to continue to make the best products in the world that delight our customers and make our employees incredibly proud of what they do."

Today, Apple is vastly more prominent and more complex than the computer company that Jobs stepped away from. It has many interests in a wide variety of products, services, and markets. In a *Wired* article titled "Why Tim Cook is a better Apple CEO than Steve Jobs," the author makes a compelling case that Cook is better suited to run Apple in ways that Jobs was not. The proof, he argues, is in the numbers. Apple is the world's first trillion-dollar company, a milestone achieved under Cook's leadership. And during his tenure, Cook almost tripled Apple's revenue. In 2018 Apple earned $265.6 billion, the highest annual revenue in the company's history.

How did this happen? Cook maximized Jobs's approach to innovation and embraced change time and again. Additionally, he exemplified progressive values such as diversity, inclusion, and privacy. And he continues to champion the company's renewed environmental commitment.

Consider that at the time of Jobs's death in 2011, Greenpeace's Greener Electronics Guide gave the company a score of just under five out of ten in its commitment to the environment. Since Cook started leading the company, Apple has invested billions in green power and is now running on 100 percent renewable energy worldwide. Additionally, it's the only tech company committed to making its supply chain 100 percent sustainable. Why do this, even though the costs could hurt the company's bottom line in the immediate future? Because Cook sees the world that will be and is preparing Apple to meet the future at an opportune moment. More often than not, this involves renewing aspects of the organization or the organization altogether—a difficult undertaking, but one that continues to allow Apple to grow and maintain its market dominance.

Follow Tim Cook's lead: Know that leadership is a values-based system of action. While you adjust your priorities and strategies, your core values must remain unshakable.

Amid all this adulation for change-friendly leaders, you might be wondering, *What about consistency? What about doing something correctly, for as long as possible?* I'm going to stake a claim, based on the few examples I've offered thus far, as well as the dozens more in this book alone: The only constant is constant change. Now, more than ever, our world is changing. Quite literally, no one can afford to stay the same.

Consistency in VUCA times can prove counterproductive. I used to believe in the adage "nothing changes if nothing changes." But now I'm convinced that, in our fast-paced and ever-changing world, something *does* change if nothing changes: trajectory.

If you assume that not making changes will keep you on the same upward trajectory, you're in for an inevitable, unpleasant surprise. Our external environment is simply too volatile, uncertain, complex, and ambiguous—so much so that if you fail to prepare, then prepare to fail.

The onus is on us, as leaders of our respective organizations, to fathom the future. Instead of avoiding it, pretending that we're somehow exempt from it, we must meet the future with eyes wide open.

"Nothing is more powerful than an idea whose time has come."

— VICTOR HUGO
(Poet and novelist)

CHAPTER 2

Inclusion and Diversity Challenges in Leadership

In his book, *Super Pumped: The Battle for Uber*, author Mike Isaac describes how Jeff Jones—the person responsible for Uber's public perception—assembled a group of executives from across Uber's different divisions to review the results of the brand. Jones discovered that Uber didn't have an image problem—it had a leadership problem. Sentiment toward CEO Travis Kalanick was plummeting amid reports of sexual harassment, mismanagement, and an overall toxic company culture. Though consumers loved the brand, Kalanick's negative profile was actively undermining it. How bad was the damage? The entire debacle—including a six-minute video released by Bloomberg News that showed Kalanick yelling at an UberBlack driver—saw the company's valuation free-fall from $72 billion down to $48 billion . . .

It's hard to imagine a world without Uber. But as impactful and enormous as the company was under Travis Kalanick's leadership, Uber's obsolescence was a genuine possibility. By failing to champion diversity and inclusion, Kalanick inadvertently produced a drought of diverse thoughts at the company—the very thoughts that could have yielded the better, more creative, and more innovative problem solving that would have helped Uber avoid obsolescence in the first place. In order to understand how to break free from these destructive patterns and reinvent for the future, we need to better understand our past.

Consider the Fortune Global 500, published by *Fortune* magazine, which ranks 500 of the largest corporations in the world by total revenue for their respective fiscal years. In 2019, these were the top 10 companies on that list:

1. Walmart
2. Sinopec Group
3. Royal Dutch Shell
4. China National Petroleum
5. State Grid
6. Saudi Aramco
7. BP
8. ExxonMobil
9. Volkswagen
10. Toyota Motor

Twenty-four years earlier, in 1995, the top 10 companies on that list were these:

1. Mitsubishi Corporation
2. Mitsui & Co., Ltd.
3. Itochu Corporation
4. Sumitomo Corporation
5. General Motors Corporation

6.	Marubeni Corporation	9.	Nissho Iwai Corporation
7.	Ford Motor Company	10.	Royal Dutch/Shell Group
8.	Exxon Corporation		

And when we rewind the clock even further, all the way to 1955, the top 10 list looked like this:

1.	General Motors	6.	Chrysler
2.	Exxon Mobil	7.	Armour
3.	US Steel	8.	Gulf Oil
4.	General Electric	9.	Mobil
5.	Esmark	10.	DuPont

Compare all three lists. Do you notice that none of the listings are identical? And here's where it gets even more interesting: Of the 500 companies listed in 1955, only 12 appear on the 2019 list. This means that in 65 years, a whopping 88 percent of Fortune Global 500 companies were dissolved, went bankrupt, or got acquired. The first *Fortune* rankings came out in 1917. How many companies would you estimate, from way back in 1917, are still on the Fortune Global 500 list today? Take a wild guess.

One. And I'll reveal who, but more importantly, *why*, by the end of this book.

The bleak truth about organizations is this: Most of them fail. Time has swallowed corporate, government, and social enterprises that neither planned to change *as* necessary nor change the plan *when* necessary. Organizations must learn to adapt, or else they lapse into irrelevance. This shouldn't be surprising, yet leaders continuously fail to navigate change. What might explain this recurrence?

Let's turn to *Fortune* again for an answer. In 2002, their research division published a report in which they outlined 10 reasons why organizations collapse:

1. **Success stifles decision-making.** Following periods of continual success, leaders become complacent and prone to poor judgment.

2. **Employees fear the boss more than the competition.** Leaders are unable to receive complete information because it's withheld by fearful employees. Worse, employees are trained to lie to their superiors.

3. **Too much risk-taking.** Believing that victory is imminent, some organizations live too close to the edge by over-spending and over-leveraging themselves.

4. **Acquisition lust.** Leaders grow intoxicated by the rush of acquiring new assets (such as employees, technology, or other organizations) and neglect to optimize their existing ones.

5. **Listening to Wall Street more than to employees.** Leaders mistake stock prices as drivers of success instead of by-products of success.

6. **Following the strategy du jour.** Wooed by trends and gimmicks, organizations chase one shiny ball after another without much consideration.

7. **A dangerous corporate culture.** With no one comfortable enough to raise questions, the organization's broken moral compass leads to reckless and unethical behavior. Nortel, Salomon Brothers, and Arthur Andersen are prime examples of this pitfall.

8. **Floating on "new economy" hot air.** The company over-estimates the value of inherently fragile conceptual assets (such as intellectual property) over physical assets (such as machinery and production facilities).

9. **A dysfunctional board.** All too often, board members remain beholden to management. As in the case of Theranos, they can sometimes devolve into mere window dressing.

10. **Seeing no evil.** Organizations engage in avoidance—they're slow to confront the changing world around them. And by failing to reinvent themselves, they succumb to inevitable entropy.

Dig up any case study of a defunct company from recent history (e.g., RadioShack, Toys"R"Us, WOW air, Vertu, etc.). Then run it through *Fortune*'s list. You'll likely end up with a handful of reasons why the company is no more. But revisit several case studies, and you'll notice that one factor appears to be consistent across all of them. And that's *avoidance*: a failure to confront that which confronts you.

In our VUCA world, the volume and frequency of brutal facts facing companies from both within and without are overwhelming. Here's a quick assessment of just how our world is changing, according to the 2019 World Economic Forum briefing:

Disruption is intensifying. Powerful forces such as emerging economies and artificial intelligence are changing our world, impacting everything from countries to companies and their employees to the environment.

The gulf between those embracing change and those falling behind is growing. Inequality is growing among countries, companies, and individuals, which is contributing to an increase in political and social discontent.

We're moving toward a more inclusive society. There has been a reconfiguration of the definition of "success" to be more inclusive and sustainable, meaning that more people will benefit from future economic growth.

Modern leaders must remain prepared to respond to change faster than ever before. For careless leaders, avoidance of the changing world obscures reality. These leaders fail to see the extent to which internal and/or external environments have shifted. By the time their organization arrives at an inflection point, it's already too late, and the organization is in a state of decline.

Even those leaders who acknowledge the changes that are coming and seem sufficiently prepared to change can succumb to catastrophic missteps. What sabotages their good intentions? Two words: *active inertia.*

"Active inertia" essentially means to mindlessly follow established patterns of behavior instead of considering alternatives, even when times are changing. Because a particular strategy or procedure worked in the past, leaders go back to it again and again, thinking it will solve current problems. Instead it seals their doom. Think Borders opening up more bookstores while users flocked to Amazon; the Recording Industry Association of America suing Napster while digital downloads outpaced physical sales; or Xerox doubling down on copy machines while businesses were going digital.

In a 1999 *Harvard Business Review* article, Donald Sull, senior lecturer at the MIT Sloan School of Management, presented four areas where active inertia can take hold. These should serve as warning signs that a company is doomed to make the wrong decision at the fourth (and possibly final) stage of a business cycle if it's unwilling to make changes in these key areas:

1. **Strategic frames:** Assumptions that determine how leaders view the organization. Unexamined, they become blinders. For instance, Polaroid's leadership grew overconfident

enough to disregard the effect of digital cameras on their business.

2. **Processes:** Doing things based on the way they were previously done. Unexamined, they become routines. For instance, General Motors blatantly ignored their competition and doubled down on their existing and outdated manufacturing processes.

3. **Relationships:** Ties to employees, customers, suppliers, distributors, and shareholders. Unexamined, they become shackles. For instance, Toys"R"Us signed a losing deal with Amazon rather than building their own platform.

4. **Values:** Shared beliefs that determine corporate culture. Unexamined, they lead to dogmas. For instance, Blockbuster shunned Netflix's online gamble, believing that the only way to survive in the industry would be through operating physical stores.

Strategic frames, processes, relationships, and values are essential components of an effective organization. But when they devolve into blinders, routines, shackles, and dogmas, the end is imminent.

Perhaps the most important takeaway is this: It's all well and good to carefully plan out a change management initiative, but leaders need to begin transforming their organizations by transforming themselves. A successful organizational transformation requires that the leader undergo a personal transformation. Succumbing to active inertia, Uber's Travis Kalanick refused to reinvent himself as a leader in accordance with the changing world around him. And as a result, he developed a major blind spot concerning the power of diversity and inclusion to visualize and realize change before it happens.

The Changing Landscape of Leadership

To successfully lead an organization in the future depends on a leader's willingness to embrace change in the present. Whether you're a leader in a corporation, government, or not-for-profit, the only constant in your role will be constant change.

Consider the four major industrial revolutions and how they have influenced every subsequent era of work.

The First Industrial Revolution (1765): Mechanization displaced traditional agriculture, eventually becoming the backbone of the societal economy. The enormous extraction of coal and the invention of the steam engine would dramatically increase the speed of manufacturing, further accelerating the economy.

The Second Industrial Revolution (1870): New sources of energy—electricity, gas, and oil—would culminate in the creation of the internal combustion engine. Simultaneous advancements in metallurgy, chemical synthesis, and methods of communication would catalyze quantum leaps in societal evolution. Specifically, the inventions of the automobile and the aircraft at the end of the 20th century propelled us into the future.

The Third Industrial Revolution (1969): The rise of yet another source of untapped energy: nuclear. And concurrently, the rise of electronics, telecommunications, and computers. New industries were born, including space expeditions, research, and biotechnology.

The Fourth Industrial Revolution: At the time of this book's writing (and most likely at the time of your reading) we are living through this revolution. This era brought us the internet. And with it, the rapid succession of technological phenomena.

As we touched on earlier, approaches to leadership have changed as well. In the First Industrial Revolution, commercial organizations achieved unprecedented scale, and managers were needed to handle this growth. By the early 1900s, management as a practice had become widely accepted. And by the mid-20th century, the practice continued to become more refined and crystallized. Each revolution was a catalyst for change, producing new and different ways of leading. Through these changes, seven distinct leadership styles seem to have stuck:

1. **Democratic leadership:** The leader takes input from everyone on the team to make decisions.

2. **Autocratic leadership:** The opposite of democratic leadership. A remnant of the First Industrial Revolution, this style of leadership is grossly outdated and incompatible with today's knowledge workers.

3. **Laissez-faire leadership:** The leader offers direction only when absolutely necessary. A hands-off approach; the French term "laissez-faire" translates as "let them do."

4. **Strategic leadership:** A balance of the organization's needs and the needs of the employees. (For example, Airbnb's modern leader, Brian Chesky, made the difficult decision to lay off 25 percent of his company's workforce in 2020. This was clearly gut-wrenching for Chesky, but as a strategic leader, he had to do what was necessary to keep the company alive.)

5. **Transformational leadership:** In recent times, this style has gained considerable traction. The transformational leader strives to continually "transform" and improve the company, pushing everyone outside their comfort zone.

6. **Transactional leadership:** Leadership that rewards employees precisely for the amount of work they do: no more, no less.

7. **Coach-style leadership:** This leader focuses on building up the strengths and skills of individuals, while also focusing on ways that everyone can work better together.

Other changes accompany and influence the changing landscape of leadership—like technology. According to the law of accelerating returns, "The pace of technological progress (especially information technology) speeds up exponentially over time because there is a common force driving it forward." Our technology compels us to evolve, and we, in turn, innovate, bringing forth new technology. And through this reciprocal process, new technology informs the zeitgeist—the so-called spirit of the age or spirit of the times, as the concept was first defined in 18th- and 19th-century German philosophy. As the zeitgeist shifts, so do we—we change it, and in turn, it changes us.

In the last decade, we've seen many critical upheavals play out in the zeitgeist. Viral ideas spread, and imbalanced equations demanded resolution: In countries like India and America, we saw nationalism crawl through the cracks of globalism, and we saw the disenfranchised pillory the privileged. In 2019, our zeitgeist contained some undeniable markers that signaled our world was clamoring for change: NFL quarterback-turned-activist Colin Kaepernick's iconic protest was followed by Jay-Z's strategic partnership with the NFL, resulting in a politically charged halftime show. And the powerful sentiments undergirding this small handful of examples erupted in the form of the convulsive global protests triggered by the senseless murders of George Floyd, Ahmaud Arbery, and Breonna Taylor.

Our world already feels plenty volatile, uncertain, complex, and ambiguous. But the rate of change is only going to increase, in lockstep with the pace of technological evolution—especially information technology. Therefore, it's critical that a modern leader have a solid grasp of not just their internal environment (themselves, their teams, their company culture, and so on) but also a strong understanding of their external environment (including social shifts, economic shifts, their competitive landscape). Outdated modes of leadership—avoidant, aggressive, and autocratic—are marred with blind spots. They sabotage the required insight and foresight necessary to maneuver through an ever-changing zeitgeist.

Let's further explore how a leader's blind spots and active (or passive) engagement in avoidant behavior can prove destructive.

Leadership Trends in Recent Times

The 2020s began on a VUCA note. The decade that preceded it witnessed the Amazon and much of Australia engulfed in wildfires; the polarization and hardening of political ideologies and resurgence of nationalism; failures in technology governance such as those unearthed by the likes of ex-CIA contractor Edward Snowden and Cambridge Analytica whistleblower Christopher Wylie; and a disorienting post-truth climate. Several communities felt increasingly neglected and distrustful of their leaders' ability to act decisively, beyond their personal interests. The Women's March, Occupy Wall Street, Black Lives Matter, National School Walkout, and several other movements were all symptomatic of this.

The most important leadership trend in our phase of the Fourth Industrial Revolution—a time characterized by exponential and sweeping social and technological change and a zeitgeist calling for a reshuffle of the deck of power—is this: The call for "business as usual" is a death sentence. Stagnation in a business's internal environment will not produce the resilience required to adapt to and withstand the external environment.

I'm aware that all this is heavy to read. Trust me, it's heavy to write. As a leader, I understand why avoidance is comforting, even tempting. Leaders sense at some level that their organizations need to be more innovative, and they suspect that it won't happen unless they're willing to share the power. But at the same time, they're fearful that the endeavor will fall into chaos if they loosen the reins. This forms the precondition for active inertia (page 32). Stubborn leaders might even experience momentary victories, which they take to indicate that the pendulum is swinging back in their direction. However, this is but an optical illusion.

As an intern at Sony Music Entertainment in 2008, I witnessed this firsthand. My supervisor pulled me aside at the end of a three-month-long internship and asked if I wanted to stick around to "see what happens next." He told me that things were about to change: the company, the industry—everything. And he was right. In one year, I watched as the company hemorrhaged personnel. Entire teams and divisions were gutted. The rise of streaming services, the decline of physical sales, and the global economic crisis all played a role in why this traditional record label had to rebuild itself.

But what truly did the organization in was avoidance: Its leaders simply stopped paying attention. In fact, the writing was on the wall for years before I showed up. From 2000 to 2003, every major label reported a consistent decline in physical sales. A year later, there was a small blip of growth in physical sales (the aforementioned "optical illusion"), followed by a sharp plummet over the next four years. And during those four years, digital sales soared.

By the time I showed up, it was undeniable: Physical sales were out, digital sales were in. Yet, the leadership insisted on stamping CDs while sometimes dismissing downloads and streaming as a fad. And it's not as though people didn't speak up and raise the alarm. Plenty, including my supervisor, were vocal. But whether or not leadership was listening is questionable.

How do leaders avoid this scenario? *The Global Leadership Forecast 2018* was one of the most expansive leadership research projects ever conducted. Integrating data from more than 28,000 leaders and HR professionals at 2,488 organizations around the world, this report makes it resoundingly clear that organizations need to focus on cultural factors to improve their leaders' ability to respond to disruption. As reported on Forbes.com, it outlines three aspects of progressive company culture in particular:

1. **Informing decisions through data and analytics.** To leverage the power of big data, machine learning, artificial intelligence, and other technologies to better understand and respond to shifting environments.

2. **Integrating multiple diverse perspectives to drive change.** To cease overreliance on the same voices and viewpoints that are usually considered, and to make space for those with different (and contrarian) voices and viewpoints.

3. **Embracing failure in pursuit of innovation.** To regard failure as an indication that progress is being made toward organizational reinvention, rather than playing it safe only to face certain demise later.

In other words, taking in diverse points of view—whether it's multiple data sets, varied perspectives from team members, or the lessons to be learned from failure—wins the day.

Valuing diversity fits with the zeitgeist and technology we're living with. The internet and the critical mass of social media makes it impossible to limit our exposure to the broad and diverse realities of our world. Whether you're in Charleston, South Carolina, or Chennai, Tamil Nadu; whether you identify as a straight woman or nonbinary; our diverse human gradient is both undeniable and unavoidable like never before.

Unfortunately, our brains haven't had any significant upgrades over the last 10,000 years. We retain our instinct to distrust strangers who don't look and act like we do. As a result, avoidant leaders tend to conflate "cultural fit" with "comfortable fit" and hire people just like themselves. Claudio Fernández-Aráoz, author of the book *Great People Decisions*, expands on this point, writing that, "Similarity, familiarity, and comfort were the right criteria for survival people choices over the millennia. Unfortunately, they are today the exact opposite of what we need to set up great teams with complementary skills and the ability to properly challenge each other."

Time and time again, research validates the notion that diversity of thought leads to better, more creative, more innovative problem-solving. And diversity of thought almost always correlates to the diversity of people.

Let's take a look at the state of leadership when it comes to women, the LGBTQIA+ community, and people of color.

Women in Leadership

When my predecessor at Ryerson University hired me to take on the role of digital community facilitator—a role that involved creating and fostering a sense of online community among a decentralized and commuter campus—he had essentially hired someone with a skill set and mindset similar to his own. Later, when it came time for me to choose my own successor, I went about the selection process in much the same way, searching for another digital marketing specialist with an entrepreneurial flair. But there was a slight problem. Under my leadership, the RU Student Life online community's growth had stagnated. It required a refresh, perhaps even an overhaul. And I suspected that we wouldn't get it by doing what we had always done.

Enter my successor, Tesni Ellis, a deeply empathetic and emotionally intelligent storyteller by both passion and profession, who intimately understood the power of compelling storytelling. Under her leadership, Tesni reinvigorated the RU Student Life brand by increasing its focus on telling better student stories. This model continues to be replicated across the country (and around the world) to this day. Where I developed tunnel vision, Tesni was open-minded; where I was losing touch, she was highly attuned; where I was moody, she was empathetic. Tesni was able to improve upon my prototype of leadership and move the brand further than ever. Had I hired another "me," RU Student Life would've likely continued to stagnate. And as you know by now, stagnation leads to ruin.

Despite the obstacles they faced (more about those in a moment) we have many examples of skillful, effective, and innovative women leaders. In politics and governance, examples include Eleanor Roosevelt, Madeleine Albright, and Ruth Bader Ginsburg. In the business world, high-profile leaders include beauty product maven Elizabeth Arden; Sheryl Sandburg, COO of Facebook; and General Motors CEO and chair Mary Barra. Oprah Winfrey, Taylor Swift, and Beyoncé have transcended their marquee careers, combining talent and savvy to become brands in their own right. And yet when it comes to empowering women to take on leadership roles, there's still more work to be done.

CHALLENGES AND BARRIERS

As of January 1, 2020, only 37 of the Fortune 500 CEOs identify as women. And only three years prior, there were 15 women world leaders in office—out of about 195 nations—8 of whom were their country's first woman in power. And considering that women have been allowed to vote in the United States only since 1920, we see a bigger, structural problem: systemic barriers to women's full partici-pation in leadership.

There's hardly a shortage of qualified women to occupy leadership roles. Consider that in the United States, women make up almost half of the total labor force. And though they outnumber men in earning degrees, they are less likely to rise to the highest paying and most coveted leadership roles. According to research published by the World Data Bank, globally less than half of all women participated in the labor force in 2019. In fact, this number represents a decrease since 1990. By comparison, nearly 75 percent of men participated in the labor force in 2019. Despite an increase in women pursuing higher education globally, and as a result of both structural barriers and cultural restrictions, this alarming gender gap remains among highly educated women and men in some countries. For instance, unpaid caregiving responsibilities can prevent paid employment opportunities, and this work disproportionately falls on the shoulders of women. Globally, only 1.5 percent of men provide unpaid childcare on a full-time basis, compared to 606 million (21.7 percent) of women.

Let's take a closer look. The American Association of University Women is a nonprofit organization that advances equity for women through advocacy, education, and research. In a 2020 report titled "Barriers and Bias: The Status of Women in Leadership," they outlined four distinct ways that outdated leadership models shut women out:

1. **Old stereotypes.** Traditional power structures tend to value traits considered masculine (such as power and assertiveness), but frown on them when they're exhibited by women.

2. **Fewer connections.** Men continue to benefit more than women in terms of opportunities for advancement due to their disproportionate access to networks, mentorship, and sponsorship.

3. **Bias and discrimination.** The persistence of sexual harassment, toxic work environments, and unconscious bias continue to perpetuate gender discrimination in the workplace.

4. **Lack of flexibility balancing.** Sadly, workplaces are still designed around outdated notions of domestic roles. This further prevents women from attaining leadership roles.

Companies who aren't addressing these issues will suffer from a lack of diversity, and therefore a lack of innovation. The job site Glassdoor.com found that 67 percent of job seekers consider a prospective employer's workforce diversity when evaluating a job offer. And a recent survey by multinational consulting firm PwC found that 61 percent of women consider the gender diversity of the employer's leadership team when evaluating a potential workplace.

TRIUMPHS

Despite the barriers they've faced—and continue to face—women in leadership positions, especially those empowered through intentional inclusion, have been able to shift our world.

Think about teenage sensation Greta Thunberg, who sailed from Sweden to New York City to protest climate change at the United Nations. The 16-year-old's bold act inspired a global teenage strike. Thunberg was later named *Time*'s Person of the Year, and she remains an icon of the climate change movement. Or consider Reshma Saujani, an American lawyer and politician, who was the first Indian-American woman (and the first South Asian–American woman) to run for U.S. Congress. Saujani, as the founder and CEO of Girls Who Code, gave free computer science education to more than 40,000 young women in the United States.

There are also examples like Ginni Rometty, who became the first woman to serve as chairman, president, and CEO of IBM. During her tenure, she reinvented more than 50 percent of IBM's portfolio, built a $21 billion hybrid cloud business, and established IBM's leadership in AI, quantum computing, and blockchain. And Angela Merkel, chancellor of Germany, navigated that nation through back-to-back crises as she helped her country become Europe's leading power for the first time since World War II. Merkel also ushered in a golden period for Europe's largest economy, pushing unemployment to its lowest levels since the early 1980s.

None of these accomplishments should be surprising. Time and again, significant research has made the connection between diversity and innovation. Research by Sylvia Hewlett, Melinda Marshall, and Laura Sherbin, for example, concluded that diverse leaders were more inclined to create an environment where new, creative ideas were considered—the kind of ideas that prepare an organization to thrive in the future.

REFLECTIONS

Finland's prime minister Antti Rinne resigned in December of 2019 after a party of the ruling coalition said they had lost confidence in Rinne following a series of disruptive strikes. His successor, 34-year-old Sanna Marin, represents a complete departure from Rinne's style of leadership.

For starters, it's well-documented that Rinne's lack of collaboration cost him trust with the government. Marin, on the other hand, has made collaboration a central tenet of her leadership. Whereas Rinne surrounded himself with men who shared his guarded and secretive approach to governance, Marin surrounded herself with women and promoted an open and transparent approach to governance. Especially when contrasted with her obstinate male predecessor, Sanna Marin's efficacy as a leader speaks to the importance of women in the future of work—a future in which compassion and collaboration are essential.

A 2013 study by the National Bureau of Economic Research confirmed that women find collaboration more appealing than men do. Some men favor team-oriented work environments only if they believe that approach would be more efficient. Research also shows that men statistically tend to have a pessimistic view of their teammates' potential abilities. It follows that in an increasingly diverse, connected, and collaborative workforce, the exclusion of women can have an adverse effect on productivity and long-term success.

The future of work demands a more human-centric and change-friendly approach to getting things done. It requires trust and collaboration, not fear and hoarding. Achieving equitable and sustainable outcomes simply can't happen when leadership is homogenous, especially in terms of gender.

LGBTQIA+ Community in Leadership

I'll admit—the concept of "bring your whole self to work" confused me at first. I thought I already did bring my whole self to work. Then I met Dr. John Austin, executive director of Student Affairs at Ryerson University. One of Dr. Austin's first orders of business was to unlock the diversity contained in the human gradient of his staff. He began this campaign at a town hall meeting. After sharing a candid story about his experiences as a gay man, he beckoned to the team to bring their whole selves to work—for each of us to express our identity fully and freely. And he promised to continue doing the same.

Was I not already bringing my whole self to work? I thought afterward. The truth is, I wasn't. How could I? I grew up in mostly lower-income neighborhoods, the Muslim son of Indian immigrant parents, intersectionalities that I mistakenly believed to work against me. Fearing stigma, I concealed my struggles with mental illness, a failed engagement, and drug and alcohol abuse. And on top of that, I had been a military reservist for several years, where my very identity had been stamped out in service of being a part of the collective. All I knew until that point of my career was how not to be myself—and to be only the part of myself that was productive. And while my experiences aren't nearly the same as someone who identifies as LGBTQIA+, I understand what it feels like to not feel able to express myself fully and freely, and how important it is to be able to do so.

Alan Turing, a British mathematician and scientist, played a critical role in breaking the code for the Nazi Enigma machine in World War II, assisting in the defeat of Adolf Hitler and the resolution of the war. Months after he broke the code, however, the British government arrested the closeted Turing on the charge of "gross inadequacy" under the Criminal Law Amendment Act—the same charge used against Oscar Wilde. Turing was chemically castrated after information about his relationship with another man became known. He committed suicide two years later. Imagine if Turing had been empowered to bring his whole self to work and continue his career, rather than discard it. What other innovations might he have produced? We'll never know. But we can work hard today to make sure that more of the human gradient is recognized and empowered.

Like women, the LGBTQIA+ community has been systematically prohibited from exploring and unlocking their talents in the workplace. While there were only 33 female CEOs represented on the 2019 Fortune 500 list, there were only 3 CEOs who publicly identified as LGBTQIA+. The numbers around the world aren't promising either. Only 7 of the globe's 1,645 billionaires openly identify as LGBTQIA+. And in recorded history, there have been only 5 openly LGBTQIA+ world leaders. We have to do better.

CHALLENGES AND BARRIERS

While several countries around the world prohibit discrimination in employment because of sexual orientation, only five—Bolivia, Ecuador, Fiji, Malta, and the UK—have a constitutional guarantee of equality for citizens on the basis of sexual orientation and gender identity, according to a 2016 UCLA study. Forget about not being given an equal opportunity to discover, explore, and maximize their gifts—a heartbreakingly large contingent of the LGTBQIA+ community never even gets a chance to enter the workforce, let alone become leaders. Worse, most countries and states do not provide legal protections for LGBTQIA+ employees.

Employees who do identify as LGBTQIA+ often face hostility in the workplace. According to a groundbreaking study by the Robert Wood Johnson Foundation and the Harvard T.H. Chan School of Public Health, one in five LGBTQIA+ job-seeking Americans has experienced discrimination based on their sexual orientation or gender identity. The very same study showed that people of color who identify as LGBTQIA+ tend to experience this type of discrimination more than their white counterparts. It's also been reported that 22 percent of LGBTQIA+ Americans did not get the same pay raises or promotion opportunities as their peers. The numbers are even more appalling if you're a member of the trans community. A report by the National Center for Transgender Equality revealed that over a quarter of the transgender population said they were not hired, were fired, or were not promoted due to their gender identity of expression. And 80 percent of those employed reported either experiencing harassment or mistreatment on the job, or having to take steps to avoid it.

In the end, prevailing fear prevents LGBTQIA+ employees from freely expressing their full identities in the workplace. Like women and people of color, to avoid discrimination they often obscure personal relationships, code-switch or change the way they dress or speak, and avoid discussing certain aspects of their lives. According to researchers Deena Fidas and Liz Cooper, the cognitive dissonance and the constant performance of LGBTQIA+ employees result in employees feeling exhausted from spending time and energy hiding their sexual orientation and gender identity.

As with women, the deck of power is stacked very much against the LGBTQIA+ community. Yet, despite all this, tremendous progress has been made.

TRIUMPHS

Resisting and enduring deeply embedded hatred and prejudice, the LGBTQIA+ community has continued to rise and occupy leadership positions in organizations around the world. Especially when they've been appropriately empowered through intentional inclusion, these leaders have been able to change the course of history.

Consider legendary activist Harvey Milk. While not the first LGBTQIA+ person to hold public office, he was immensely influential in shaping the spirit of queer resistance even before his historic term on the San Francisco Board of Supervisors as California's first out gay politician. Or think about how America's first female astronaut, Sally Ride, a space shuttle robotic arm operator, helped pave the way for women in STEM careers. And when she came out posthumously (and subtly) in her obituary, she represented many more firsts for queer women everywhere.

Visual activist Zanele Muholi, a photographer and activist, shed light on Black queer South Africans at a time when the country ostracized the LGBTQIA+ community. And when Inga Beale (who counts Alan Turing as one of her role models) became the first-ever female CEO of Lloyd's of London in 2014, she concurrently became one of the most powerful LGBTQIA+ leaders in the world.

Matt Ryan is the former executive vice president and chief marketing officer of Starbucks Corporation. Under his leadership, he enhanced the company's customer relationship management and loyalty capabilities. He was also instrumental in integrating the company's regional brand and marketing initiatives. Starbucks is a prominent champion of the LGBTQIA+ community, and it's not accidental. When it comes to the work of diversity and inclusion, Ryan said to employees, "It's nice to see great companies taking up the torch and helping the cause. And I think no company has a better track record than Starbucks. [Diversity and inclusion] brought me here to this company . . . it's important for us to extend and build that constantly so that everybody who works here feels welcomed and included."

REFLECTIONS

Diversity must be prioritized and activated by leadership. It must move beyond lip service and grand gestures into the very spirit of the organization. And there's no better example than Dr. Austin's efforts (page 45) to create a culture where bringing one's whole self to work was encouraged. In the end, this supported the attraction, engagement, and retention of top talent—especially LGBTQIA+ superstars from rival institutions.

It shouldn't be a surprise that LGBTQIA+ employees want to work for a company that allows them to bring their authentic selves to work. But it's important to note that this preference extends beyond LGBTQIA+ employees. Research shows that the vast majority of allies (non-LGBTQIA+ individuals who support and advocate for LGBTQIA+ individuals) prefer to work for inclusive companies. One study by the Center for Talent Innovation found that a stunning 72 percent of all respondents said that if everything else is equal, they are more likely to accept a job at a company that's supportive of LGBTQIA+ employees than one that's not.

As the stakes of organizational success get higher and higher; as the gyrating vortex of this VUCA world speeds up, it's our minority communities—women, people of color, and the LGBTQIA+ community—who we can rely on to increase our organization's capacity to change.

Future generations will be more likely to embrace their full selves and enter the realms of education and the workforce with much more self-actualization, ready to discover, explore, and maximize their gifts. Leaders must be prepared for this paradigm shift. One way—and perhaps the only way—to do that is to practice diversity and be intentionally inclusive. At the very least, it must be done to keep in step with the changing consumer. Additional Center for Talent Innovation research has revealed that "teams with members whose sexual orientation matches the target consumers are much more likely to understand the market."

But beyond the measurable impact that diversity and inclusion can have on an organization, it's simply the right thing to do.

POC in Leadership

For centuries, the cries for racial justice have grown louder and louder. Most recently, on January 15, 2015, the Academy of Motion Pictures Arts and Sciences awarded all 20 acting nominations to white actors during the Oscars for the first of two consecutive years, inspiring Black activist April Reign to create the hashtag #OscarsSoWhite. In the years that followed, the world would see Jordan Peele's Black body horror *Get Out* become a critical and commercial success. And quarterback Colin Kaepernick would take a knee during the national anthem, sparking a much-needed debate about racial inequality. In 2020 (at the time of writing), protests for racial justice continued around the world. And Senator Kamala Harris, a mixed Black and Tamil woman, ran (and ended up winning the election) for vice president of the United States of America.

While surveying today's leadership landscape, it's clear to see that modern leaders of color—those who value servitude, innovation, diversity, and empathy—are guiding organizations into the future. At the time of writing this book, Sundar Pichai is leading Google, while Marvin Ellison is leading Lowe's; Ajay Banga is leading Mastercard while Anthony Tan is leading Grab. The list goes on.

We know that diversity of thought leads to better, more creative, more innovative problem solving. And diversity of thought almost always correlates to the diversity of people. By excluding people of color from leadership, we are inhibiting our ability to innovate.

Much more work needs to be done, especially when you consider a Harvard study that exposed how non-white ethnic minorities hold only 10 percent of directorships among the nearly 20,000 positions it reviewed.

CHALLENGES AND BARRIERS

Although the number of Fortune 500 companies with over 40 percent diversity has more than doubled from 69 to 145 since 2012, as of 2020 there are only four Black CEOs leading Fortune 500 companies.

As a person of color, thriving in the future of work can require paying a steep invisible tax. It may involve overcoming such things as blatant racism, unconscious bias, regressive cultural norms, and even learned helplessness. Leadership unattuned to this lived experience, even with good intentions, can cause considerable harm to the people of color in their organization, and to the organization itself.

Let's return to the story of Uber CEO Travis Kalanick. By mid-2017, Kalanick hired an Apple veteran, Bozoma Saint John. Saint John, a Black female executive, was chosen first and foremost for her skills—but also as a PR remedy after Uber was blasted for having a culture that wasn't inclusive. Just a year later, Saint John abruptly and unceremoniously departed Uber. When asked why she left, Saint John opened up: "When I got to Uber, I was honest in my desire to go and change essentially what I thought was a challenging environment, especially for women and for people of color," she said. "What I discovered was a lot of people who had a desire to do better, honestly, but couldn't get out of their own way." In other words, she wasn't granted the authority to make substantive changes.

We fail to unlock the capabilities of the full human gradient when we don't include people of color on our teams. And while adding diversity to an organization is vital, it's meaningless to build a diverse workforce if you don't activate and empower them. Diversity without inclusion is just as ineffective as a lack of diversity in the first place. Diversity advocate Vernā Myers explains it this way: "Diversity is being invited to the party. Inclusion is being asked to dance." Saint John's addition to Uber's team was pointless if she wasn't empowered to truly shake things up.

Properly empowering people of color requires significant leadership and organizational commitment. It requires meaningful one-on-one and team interactions, and actively challenging biased, racist, and xenophobic behaviors—especially in team settings. It involves tailoring support and avoiding color-blind company communications that might place excessive strain on employees of color. And it involves creating intentional spaces to uncover the experiences, sentiments, and needs of these employees.

Activating diversity through inclusion isn't easy. But the payoff isn't just worth it—it's critical.

TRIUMPHS

As for women and those who identify as LGBTQIA+, there are structural barriers to full participation for people of color. But despite the odds, we've seen major success stories.

My father, a blue-collar immigrant from India, is in awe of today's diverse leadership landscape. Any time an influential person of color makes the news, he excitedly reflects on how much the world has changed. I share his enthusiasm with the knowledge that these victories are indicative of a global shift in the right direction.

Think about rapper-turned-mogul Shawn Carter, a.k.a. Jay-Z, who has created and operated many companies, starting with Roc-A-Fella Records in 1995. From apparel to restaurants, streaming apps to champagne, Jay-Z's empire stretches far and wide. In 2019, Jay-Z struck a landmark deal with the NFL—a partnership that shook the zeitgeist, as it enabled him to program the Super Bowl halftime show and guide its charitable endeavors. Or look at Rihanna, whose Fenty beauty line (designed primarily for women of color, by a woman of color) was able to eat significant market share from billionaire competitor Kylie Jenner's beauty line. Almost overnight, Kylie and other brands began to pander to women of color by emulating Fenty's approach.

Consider Sundar Pichai, CEO of Alphabet Inc. and its subsidiary Google LLC. After he was hired as a product manager of

Google in 2004, Pichai developed Google Chrome, Chrome OS, and Google Drive. He then went on to oversee the massively popular Gmail and Google Maps product development. In 2013, Pichai became the leader of the Android operating system, which powers smartphones worldwide.

In 2018, a *New York Times* investigation reported that Google gave Android creator Andy Rubin $90 million when he left the company after being accused of sexual misconduct. In response, Google employees staged a global walkout. Rather than defend the decision or ignore the writing on the wall, Pichai expressed support for the walkout and its call for better treatment of women. He went on to send a memo to all Google employees outlining changes to how the company would handle misconduct allegations, committing to "be a representative, equitable, and respectful workplace."

Pichai knows what it's like to be in the minority; through sheer lived experience, he understands what it feels like to be relatively powerless. When a leadership moment presented itself, he instinctively knew what real (not merely cosmetic) changes he needed to make.

REFLECTIONS

In the end, Uber was able to revive itself with the help of a new leader: Iranian-American CEO Dara Khosrowshahi, who immediately set the tone for a new, improved Uber with both words and actions. Two months after he was hired, he wrote a message to Uber employees, demonstrating modern leadership qualities: "The culture and approach that got Uber where it is today is not what will get us to the next level. As we move from an era of growth at all costs to one of responsible growth, our culture needs to evolve."

Unlike Kalanick, Khosrowshahi approaches the volatility, uncertainty, complexity, and ambiguity of our world with values of SIDE (servitude, innovation, diversity, and empathy). He brought to the table what Uber needed to outlast the changes in the coming years: a more cooperative spirit, more reserve, and more grace.

The world has revealed to us the transformative impact of people of color. For leaders to ignore this is irresponsible. To truly have an impact as a leader requires operationalizing and maximizing your organization's joint intellectual potential. This includes embracing change and harnessing the full spectrum of the human gradient—not only to see change *before* it happens but to be prepared to react to it *when* environments inevitably shift.

Your ability to embrace change will allow you to make the right choices and end up on the right side of the argument. Next, let's look at the steps it takes to build a values-driven leadership substructure that will allow you to hit the ground running as a new or reinvented leader.

PART 2

STRATEGIES TO HIT THE GROUND RUNNING

"Leaders with empathy do more than sympathize with the people around them: They use their knowledge to improve companies in subtle, but important ways."

— DANIEL GOLEMAN
(Author)

CHAPTER 3

Practicing Empathy

As you begin transforming your organization to thrive in a VUCA world, prepare to transform yourself as well. Whatever the challenges of your particular leadership journey, you have four principles to guide you: the SIDE leadership values of servitude, innovation, diversity, and empathy. In these next chapters, we'll explore each of those values in turn, examining how they empower you to be a human-centric, change-friendly, and self-disrupting modern leader. By the end of this book, they'll converge to form a model of leadership that will enable you to adapt to and withstand our volatile, uncertain, complex, and ambiguous world, thrive in the future of work, and guide your organization across the chasm of time. So, let's get started with empathy.

We begin this exploration—out of acronym order—by spotlighting the value of empathy. The ability to understand and share the feelings of another bears discussing first because it's a value that's highly effective but also challenging to develop, especially for new leaders rushing to succeed. Next, we'll reveal how servitude can dramatically enhance a team's performance. We'll then expand on the power of diversity and inclusion to unlock human potential. Our exploration of the bright SIDE values will end with a discussion of innovation and its importance in preparing organizations for the future.

To start, let's look at what happens when empathy is absent. In December of 2019, The Verge published an exposé titled "Emotional Baggage" in which former employees of the luggage start-up Away detailed how their CEO, Steph Korey, fostered a toxic workplace environment. Examples included firing employees who were part of an LGBTQIA+ private chat group about the workplace, as well as Korey ranting in a Slack message that whoever was in charge of a failed task must be "brain dead." The report further described Away's corporate culture as "cutthroat." It exposed how bosses would demand long hours, with little paid time off or overtime, and regularly dress down employees for such things as not answering messages immediately—even at night and on weekends.

Days after the investigation was published and went viral, Korey stepped down as CEO. Negative reviews of Away on Glassdoor, as early as 2018, had already suggested Korey's carefully crafted public persona as a modern leader to be a facade. They painted a picture of an authoritarian leader severely lacking in empathy. One former employee summed up the festering problem at the company: "A mean-girl culture that makes it a toxic environment," the review stated.

Around the time of the Away scandal, the World Health Organization upgraded the definition of burnout as "resulting from chronic workplace stress that has not been successfully managed." Having explored the concept extensively for my first book *The Burnout Gamble*, I grew curious about the role that leadership plays in creating workplace conditions that allow burnout to occur. I wondered if there was a direct link between Korey's autocratic leadership style, employee burnout, and the actions that ultimately led to the CEO's unceremonious exit. What I stumbled upon was startling.

In a 2002 edition of the *Journal of Research in Personality*, University of British Columbia researchers Delroy Paulhus and Kevin Williams introduced the concept of the "dark triad." In their groundbreaking study, the researchers sought to clarify the existing literature on personalities that are abhorrent but still within the normal range of functioning. They found that three variables were most prominent: narcissism, Machiavellianism, and psychopathy. In a report titled "Can Dark Triad Leaders Be a Good Choice for a Leadership Position?" global leadership advisory firm Egon Zehnder effectively summarized the literature to describe the personality traits that comprise the dark triad:

- **Machiavellianism:** Master manipulators, Machiavellians have little commitment to any ideology besides their own power, status, and success.

- **Narcissism:** Grandiose and self-absorbed, narcissists crave recognition and become aggressive or dominant if denied.

- **Psychopathy:** The most antisocial of the three, psychopaths are callous, risk-taking bullies who lack empathy and have problems with self-control. They can even be violent.

Paulhus and Williams's framework explains how while some dark triad leaders are praised as visionaries and role models, others can destroy entire companies.

When healthy analogs of the above traits are maximized within the normal range of functioning—like strategic thinking, confidence, and boldness—we see the likes of Barack Obama, Bill Gates, or Elon Musk operating at their most effective. But over time these leadership traits can turn malevolent, yielding such leaders as Adam Neumann (WeWork), Dov Charney (American Apparel), and Elizabeth Holmes

(Theranos). Devoid of empathy, these leaders slide toward authoritarianism and the anachronistic command-and-control style of leadership. Narcissistic leaders tend to impair the quality of team decisions by inhibiting information exchange; Machiavellian leaders tend to abuse their leadership position for their personal interests; and psychopathic leaders tend to focus on strengthening their position while implementing a climate of fear.

We now understand that financial success can mask the darkness below the surface. Social media, in particular, can be credited with giving us alternative information and smoke-and-mirrors tactics like carefully crafted press releases and flowery corporate wellness policies. The Verge's report on Steph Korey, Bloomberg's dashcam video of Travis Kalanick, and ABC's podcast about Elizabeth Holmes all gave us glimpses of how the dark triad can undermine effective leadership.

These examples make it clear that leaders who lack empathy—who withhold information and create barriers—are merely ignoring the inevitable. They avoid problems, choosing deliberately to obscure the organization's distance from its inevitable inflection point. They seem to be leaders only in title—positional leaders, if you will. They choose to turn away from the things that are facing them, which is not true leadership.

As a modern leader, it's imperative that you get real about your organization's internal and external environments. This requires a raw, no-nonsense, and distinctly human approach: empathy. In the words of author Daniel Pink, empathy is about "standing in someone else's shoes, feeling with his or her heart, seeing with his or her eyes." It's about developing true alignment with the world around you. As you've learned so far, a leader literally cannot afford to lie to themselves. To avoid becoming the naked, parading emperor, you should upgrade your leadership substructure—the style of leadership you employ—with empathy. This practice will not only allow you to see change well before it happens, because you'll understand what it is your customers are seeing and feeling, but empathy also has the multiplying effect of creating authentic human connections among your team members. These connections are essential to synchronizing an organization's efforts and success.

By operationalizing and maximizing the leadership value of empathy, you'll create the sort of accommodating organizational culture that flourishes. Let's look at some specific steps you can take.

Understand Your Environment

If you think evaluating an organization's external environment is complicated, wait until you try to assess the internal environment of an organization with a toxic culture.

To understand how the aforementioned dark triad personalities can destroy organizations from the inside, we'll turn to a 2007 paper entitled "The Toxic Triangle." Researchers Art Padilla, Bob Hogan, and Robert Kaiser explain that three factors enable this to happen:

Destructive leaders: At the top of the triangle is the toxic leader, with their dark triad traits. This leader is avoidant, aggressive, and/or authoritarian.

Susceptible followers: Conformers and colluders enable the leader's dysfunction. Conformers are passive and gain security from following an authority figure. Colluders are more proactive, actively complying with and enabling toxic leadership, and will imitate it themselves.

Conducive environment: An atmosphere that allows a toxic leader can thrive. Four elements contribute to this: instability (disorder that invites rapid, unilateral decision-making), perceived threat (an external influence that creates a sense of being under attack), questionable values and standards (or none whatsoever), and an absence of governance (any other leaders are either negligent or incompetent).

These three elements influence one another to result in a hazardous, deteriorating organization. I saw this firsthand in the first job I took after completing my undergraduate degree. I was a growth marketer at a promising publicly traded communication technology start-up, run by a CEO with the unsavory reputation of being incredibly cantankerous. It was a fast-paced work environment, and my colleagues and I barely had any one-on-ones with senior management. The CEO's leadership style yielded a culture that had devolved into one of distrust and even resentment. Nine years later, the company filed for bankruptcy. If the right people had understood that this leader's behavior indicated a toxic environment that was going to tank the organization, disaster might have been averted.

I'm grateful for my time at that start-up because I gained a vivid understanding of what not to do as a leader. It showed me the very real consequences of toxic leadership. The whole experience cemented the importance of self-awareness and situational awareness—of constantly and strategically assessing one's environment, especially when navigating change. One of the most effective ways to develop harmony with both the inside and outside of your organization is by genuinely caring about the people around you.

A 2013 Gallup study of nearly 50,000 business units across over 190 organizations found that mission-driven organizations—those who deeply know who they are, as well as how they create value for their people (customers, employees, stakeholders)—boast greater employee retention, healthier workplace cultures, higher productivity, and better customer service. And when an organization deeply understands its inner workings and higher purpose, when it understands how the world is better for its existence, then it can unlock its true potential.

Our first tried-and-tested exercises for operationalizing the value of empathy will help you assess the environment you're functioning in, so you can see how well this value is being expressed and where there's room for improvement.

REVERSE-ENGINEER THE ORGANIZATION

An exercise that any leader (or reinvented leader, for that matter) should undertake well in advance of their leadership moment is to formulate a hypothesis of the organization they're about to lead. Start by asking yourself these questions:

- What is the organization trying to become?

- What is it now?

- What is it not?

- What is its culture?

- What do its people believe in?

- How does it impact the lives of its "end users"?

The best way to formulate your hypothesis is to articulate for yourself the organization's mission, vision, values, principles, and purpose. Make sure to communicate not what the organization *says* they are, but rather *what you observe them to be*, based on how the organization is operating in the world. Casually browse through the entity's various touch points with the public: websites, social media channels, physical spaces, and so on. Chat with their current and former employees, as well as end users.

To create a better picture of your organization and its overall strategy, answer the following questions:

Vision: What are your organization's dreams of the distant future?

» What do we want people to say about our organization 100 years from now?

» What is the perfect version of our organization?

» If we had all the resources in the world, what would be different about us?

Mission: This includes what business the organization is (or isn't) in.

> » What exactly is the business we're in?
>
> » What exactly is the business we're not in (but often get confused for)?
>
> » Who are the people we serve?

Values: This is the organization's desired culture.

> » What are the values we believe/practice that make us effective?
>
> » What are the values we believe/practice that make us likable?
>
> » What are the values we believe/practice that make us great?
>
> » To what degree do we value SIDE (servitude, innovation, diversity, empathy)?

Principles: These are the employees' set of directions.

> » How do we express our values?
>
> » What are some things that our leaders preach?
>
> » What are we passionate about?

Purpose: What is the organization's impact on the lives of its end users?

> » How do we impact the lives of our end users?
>
> » How is the world a better place because we exist?
>
> » What is the legacy we're likely to leave?

With this exercise, you'll start your new leadership journey by articulating the organization's strategy based on its present manifestation. You'll need to test this hypothesis: In the next exercise, you'll find out whether the internal and external environment line up with your assessment.

Take Action!

Following a period of casual observation, form a personal hypothesis about the organization by articulating its mission, vision, values, principles, and purpose.

EMBARK ON A LISTENING TOUR

According to a recent study by employee engagement firm Sideways 6, "More than 40 percent of junior-level workers state that they are afraid to bring ideas or concerns to upper management." This can be detrimental to any business, because without a complete picture of employee ideas and apprehensions, a leader risks missing the mark.

As a modern leader, to truly understand your organization in a useful way, you should work on understanding its internal and external environments. Begin this process as early as possible; if you can't do it during a probationary period, then do it within the first 100 days of your appointment. Starting as soon as you can will help you identify issues and address them before they have a chance to manifest into problems that are impossible to untangle.

As a leader, it's imperative that you step into your leadership moment with optimal situational awareness, with your mind and heart wide open. Schedule meetings with a full spectrum of people across the organization's value chain, from executives to frontline workers, to investors, to customers, and everyone in between (even competitors, if you can). Strive for a variety of perspectives from different functional areas of the operation, especially the organization's leadership.

To get started, ask the following questions about the organization:

- What's working?

- What's not working?

- What are our strengths?

- What are our weaknesses?

- What are the opportunities for growth?

- What are the threats to our organization?

Compile the answers, summarize them, and then use your findings to guide your first 100 days as a new leader. Evaluate the data against the previously articulated organizational mission, vision, values, principles, and purpose (pages 65 to 66). This diagnostic is critical to the organization's success, as it challenges your perception of the organization, potentially exposing blind spots. It works effectively early on, as well as throughout your leadership journey.

Remember to never stop listening. Create or invest in mechanisms to ask these questions and obtain this data regularly. The more information you have, the more situational awareness (and even self-awareness) you'll develop. As a leader, one of your responsibilities is to ensure that the rate of change inside the organization (beginning in the inner sanctum of a leader's heart and mind) exceeds the rate of change outside of the organization. And that must begin with a clear understanding of what exactly is happening on the inside and outside.

Take Action!

Learn vital information about your organization by intentionally listening to the people who compose it, as well as those who interact with it.

IDENTIFY PERCEPTION GAPS

What business is Nike in? If you answered "shoes" or "apparel," guess again. John Donahoe, Nike's new CEO (as of 2020), would tell you that Nike is all about "making sport a daily habit." How about Disney, Apple, or Coca-Cola? What business are they in? I suppose a better question would be: What are they *really* selling?

Sure, Disney sells movies, Apple sells phones, and Coca-Cola sells beverages. But when you choose to watch *Frozen* over *Trolls*, decide to buy an iPhone over a Galaxy, or choose to drink Coca-Cola over Pepsi, you're making a subconscious decision guided by something deeper. Intentionally or unintentionally, you're buying into the organization's ethos, philosophy, and promise about how your life will be different as a result of engaging with them. In other words, you're buying into their brand.

Your organization's brand is a key performance indicator. It's evidence of how well you're manifesting your vision, mission, values, principles, and purpose—and how those things are congruent with the experiences of people inside and the outside the organization.

Becoming a well-integrated, recognizable, and influential brand like Nike, Disney, Apple, or Coca-Cola requires an honest evaluation. A new leader needs to understand that a brand consists of two distinct elements: perception and experience. To break this down:

- **Perception:** How the brand sees itself, how others see the brand, and how the brand wants to be seen.

- **Experience:** The activities that the brand conducts, the interactions it has with stakeholders, and the time during which the brand exists.

It behooves you to grasp just how integrated your brand's perception is. To explore this, create three columns on a whiteboard or large piece of paper. The first column represents how the brand sees itself—how it's viewed by employees and leadership alike. The second shows how the others—customers, shareholders, competitors, etc.—see the brand. And the third covers how the brand *wants* to be seen, as imagined by its leadership but informed by employees.

Now consider how your brand is perceived, filling in each column. Scan for incongruencies: Are there gaps? If inconsistencies exist among these three perspectives, ask why. This can serve as a diagnostic tool, helping you pinpoint areas where avoidant behavior and major disconnects might exist. It also trains you to use empathy, assuming the viewpoints of various parties to better understand their thinking.

Open yourself up to feedback at all levels to make your analysis as accurate as possible. Seek out qualitative and quantitative input, and get perspectives from a wide range of people. Once you understand where gaps exist among the brand's perception, explore how the experience of the brand can be changed. What brand activities could you start, stop, or continue? How can you change your brand interactions with customers and the public?

Take Action!

Seek to understand and reconcile the three dimensions of brand perception: how the brand sees itself, how others see the brand, and how the brand wants to be seen.

Put Yourself in Someone Else's Shoes

Several years ago, one of my direct reports, Lisa, had been struggling with some problems that had utterly overwhelmed her personal life, impacting her ability to fully contribute to work.

In our weekly one-on-one, Lisa downplayed her situation. Earlier in my leadership journey, I might've seen Lisa's game face, heard her canned response of "I'm good, thanks!" and swiftly moved into discussions about operations. To do so would have been a tremendous mistake, on several levels—Lisa's productivity likely would have declined, stalling many vital projects. Lisa also probably would have burned out, jeopardizing her physical and mental health. Both outcomes would have had immediate consequences for the organization's bottom line, but even greater long-term consequences for the overall company culture. After all, why would anyone choose to work for a leader who neglects their employees?

The empathic approach to a scenario like this is for the leader to ensure that questions don't yield simple yes or no answers, and that they don't come across as adversarial. To that end, a great strategy I picked up from a mentor is to ask "why," or a similar open-ended question, up to five times as a way to get to the root cause of an issue.

I paused after Lisa replied with "I'm good, thanks!" "But how are you, really?" I asked. Lisa took a deep breath. With her eyes welling up, she began to share her troubles. All the while, I made sure to actively listen; that meant making good eye contact and acknowledging her feelings and responses.

To help your employees open up, as well as to understand their experiences better, it's always best to follow up standard responses with questions such as:

- How do you know?

- How did that make you feel?

- How did this affect you?

- What are the consequences of this?

- Why do you say that?

According to professional services network Ernst & Young, a third of full-time workers globally say that managing their work and personal life has become increasingly difficult. This stress leads to absenteeism, turnover, and healthcare expenditures, which exceeds $300 billion in lost productivity in the United States alone. The World Health Organization declared stress as "the health epidemic of the 21st century." And I'm hardly catastrophizing here: According to a *Bloomberg* report, for instance, 1,600 people die each day in China from working too hard. The price of neglecting your employees is simply too high.

Following Lisa's moment of catharsis, we adjusted priorities. I made sure to check in with her in the wake of her disclosure. I made sure to accommodate her, and once Lisa was back on her feet, she regained her position in the firmament of star employees.

As a new leader, you must forge deep human relationships with your team. With this connection, three things will happen:

1. You'll foster a healthier, more productive workplace.

2. You'll earn the trust and loyalty needed to unlock the full potential of your diverse workforce.

3. You'll gain the necessary information about yourself and your organization that can come only from your team.

To those ends, let's explore a few more ways to operationalize the value of empathy.

IMPROVE YOUR ONE-ON-ONES

The easiest way to spot a change-resistant leader is to check their calendar and see how often they have one-on-one meetings with their direct reports. If they meet less than once a month, there's a good chance they're avoiding vital information and are therefore more susceptible to sinking the organization. Being busy or overwhelmed is not an excuse for leaders to unintentionally avoid one-on-ones, as this is a slippery slope toward decline. Budgets are reflections of priorities, and calendars are budgets of time; if a leader hasn't budgeted the hours to properly connect with the people they're supposed to lead, then they're actively choosing to ignore the changing world around them. In doing so, they're risking a failure to reinvent the organization.

At the same time, frequent one-on-ones are not necessarily a guarantee of organizational success. Team management app Soapbox surveyed over 1,000 managers and employees. They found that both managers and employees agree that one-on-one meetings are important but disagree on how efficient and effective the meetings are.

The goal of a one-on-one meeting is to maintain good, open communication and allow for intentional relationship building. Here's how to do one-on-ones the right way:

For starters, one-on-ones should be weekly, and ideally the length should be about 30 minutes.

They should be pre-scheduled and private.

To make most of the time you have, meetings should be structured. I recommend the impeccable structure advocated by the management consultant firm Manager Tools:

- » **The first 10 minutes:** This is your employee's agenda. What do they want to talk about? It could be their work, their family, their pets, their hobbies, their challenges, their career, or working together. The primary focus of these meetings, after all, is them.

- » **The middle 10 minutes:** This is for you to share whatever you need to share with them. During this time, you'll probably talk about projects they are working on, what you need from them, and things you've heard from higher up in the organization.

- » **The last 10 minutes:** This last portion should be for you both to talk about the future—their career, training, development, opportunities, etc. Don't end meetings early. Instead, use the gift of time to connect on a deeper level.

If adequately implemented, one-on-ones can get the best out of your team. In addition to gaining invaluable insight into the organization, you'll be able to forge genuine, helpful, and long-lasting relationships that will have a direct impact on your bottom line.

Take Action!

Develop meaningful connections with your team through recurring, structured discussions focused on their growth and well-being.

MAKE DEEPER CONNECTIONS

According to Gallup's 2015 *State of the American Manager* report, the decisions and actions of leaders accounts for "at least 70 percent of the variance in employee engagement scores across all business units." The same study notes that disengaged employees cost companies up to $500 billion annually in productivity losses. And that's just one piece of a growing body of evidence connecting bad leadership to disengaged employees, mediocre performance, and higher attrition rates.

There is a direct link between how deeply a leader is connected with their employees and how engaged their employees feel. Simply put, infrequent and shallow connections lead to disengaged employees, while frequent and deep connections lead to engaged employees. It's that simple. Yet, leaders often neglect to form genuine, long-lasting bonds.

Instead of sticking to surface-level, water-cooler chats about mundanities like sports updates and the weather, start making deeper connections. Deeper connections require in-depth conversations, and in-depth conversations require deeper questions. Many leaders are well-intentioned but lack either the emotional intelligence or the experience necessary to have these conversations.

By avoiding deeper human connections with your team, you risk several consequences: You'll foster a toxic, unproductive workplace; you won't earn the trust and loyalty needed to unlock the full human gradient of your diverse workforce; and you won't hear the necessary information about you and your organization that can come only from your team.

Therefore, it's worthwhile to start asking the deeper questions. To paraphrase pioneering psychiatrist Carl Jung: The questions you're least willing to ask are probably the questions that need to be asked the most.

Whether in one-on-ones, group meetings, feedback surveys, or whatever feedback loops are appropriate, consider asking probing questions such as the following:

- Why did you join this particular organization?

- Are you proud to work here?

- What gets you out of bed every morning?

- Do you respect our leadership?

- What are your personal and professional dreams?

- Are we headed in the right direction?

- How am I doing as a leader?

- Where can I improve my leadership?

- How would you do things differently?

- Do you envision a future for yourself at this organization?

Don't stop there. Ask excellent follow-up questions, too. Harvard researchers analyzed more than 300 conversations and found that those who were asked more meaningful follow-up questions found the other person much more likable. When you get a response, ask follow-up questions, like the exercise on page 71. They are listed again on the next page as a reminder.

- How do you know?

- How does that make you feel?

- How does that affect you?

- What are the consequences of that?

- Why do you say that?

Help your employees help you by having deeper conversations. You'll noticeably improve culture and productivity, and you'll unearth details that will help you better motivate and support them.

Take Action!

Engage your employees by asking better questions and replacing superficial small talk with more in-depth, authentic conversations.

SHADOW YOUR TEAM

A simple insight can make a world of difference; it can shift priorities and culture. Paul Damico, CEO of Moe's Southwest Grill, told *Business Insider*: "I've realized it's okay for my employees to go slower. Especially if that means getting to know the customers' names and what's going on in their lives."

As a modern leader, it's worthwhile to invest in shadowing members of your team. The benefits of this use of empathy are many:

- It enables you to gain insight into the lives of your employees.

- It offers you a better understanding of the organization's culture.

- It grants you different perspectives on your work.

- It affords you the opportunity to reflect on your leadership.

- It allows you to experience obstacles in processes.

The Manchester Metropolitan University assembled a useful guide, in which they outline three different types of job shadowing:

1. **Observation:** In this approach, you passively study others at work. One way to do this is to sit in meetings and observe how people interact. This type of job shadowing could also involve spending time with one employee, closely watching them work, and asking questions.

2. **Regular briefings:** This approach involves shadowing others during key activities on a regular basis during the completion of a single project. This type of job shadowing offers you deep insight into multiple systems, processes, and workflows.

3. **Hands-on:** A hybrid of the first two types, this approach requires you to roll up your sleeves and simulate working alongside others. This type of job shadowing will see you immersed in a project, meaningfully contributing to its execution, and asking thoughtful questions throughout.

In a conversation with Tim Hockey, CEO of TD Ameritrade, he once told me that the higher up you climb, the easier it is to fall out of sync with the realities of your employees. A story that stuck with me from this conversation with Hockey was about a senior executive he used to work for, who was so distanced from hands-on work that on the weekends, he would build birdhouses just to "feel" something.

Before you start building birdhouses, immerse yourself in the organization by shadowing the people you serve. Among other things, it may connect you with what you liked about your profession in the first place.

Gain critical insights into your organization by temporarily immersing yourself in the day-to-day work of your employees.

LEADERSHIP TIP:
Empathy and Balance

Incorporating empathy, whether in leadership or everyday life, calls for a balanced approach. Too little empathy, and you risk subduing your employees and contributing to a culture of fear and secretiveness. Too much, however, and you risk smothering your employees and being seen as a pushover.

In his *New York Times* best-selling book, *The Dichotomy of Leadership*, retired Navy SEAL Jocko Willink describes numerous dichotomies that exist within the discipline of leadership. But none is as tricky and as central as this one: to care deeply about your people, and yet at the same time accept the risks necessary to accomplish the mission.

Willink writes: "If you are more concerned for yourself than the people that work for you, you will ultimately lose. But if you put the team first ... If you, as a leader, put others above yourself ... then you will absolutely win. That's what leadership is." However, Willink also acknowledges that internal and external environments might shift at any moment, and sometimes the needs of the mission must be put before the needs of the people.

In an unbalanced approach, with the needs of the mission put before the needs of the people, you end up with cautionary tales like a 2019 article on The Logic titled "The Inner Turmoil of Cannabis Tech Company Lift & Co." The story details how several beleaguered employees called for CEO Matei Olaru's resignation, citing concerns about his ability to lead. Olaru stayed, only to fumble his response to the global pandemic of 2020. Employees were laid off, and their firing was conducted in a very insensitive and impersonal way: via mass emails. A *Vice* article titled "This Is How We Get Laid Off Now. At Home, Alone" adds that there was no conversion with employees or follow-up about outstanding expenses, and the whole ordeal led to an atmosphere of panic.

Compare that with the balanced approach of Brian Chesky, CEO of Airbnb. Preceding individual conversations, in a heartfelt letter to his employees, Chesky woefully shared that due to the constraints of the pandemic, he would have to dismiss 1,900 of his 7,500 employees. Chesky's letter is the gold standard for the balanced approach. In it, he ensured that people didn't blame themselves. He revealed his decision-making process in great detail, while reiterating the company's mission. He strove, above all, to capture the feelings of customers and employees with his words; he thanked his employees and committed to helping their future employers see the great work they'd done.

On top of that, Chesky gifted the employees their company laptops, offered clear instructions, and made himself accessible throughout their transition. Chesky, in effect, did the opposite of what a "traditional" tech CEO like Lift & Co.'s Olaru did. He took vulnerability, uncertainty, emotion, and heart, and used them for good. Chesky exemplifies the qualities of a modern leader: an empathetic servant of the people, who will undoubtedly be able to guide his organization through one portal after another.

"Talent wins games, but teamwork and intelligence wins championships."

— MICHAEL JORDAN
(Former professional basketball player)

CHAPTER 4

Exercising Servitude

Organizations that are built to last tend to have a very peculiar structure. The boss is rarely on top. And even if they are listed at the apex of their people pyramid, in function the leader tends to be at the bottom—in service of everyone else in the organization. Servitude is about putting the needs of your people before your own. Think Martin Luther King Jr. or Sam Walton. These are leaders who, each in their own way, valued people first.

With six NBA championship victories, six NBA finals MVP wins, five NBA MVP wins, and 14 NBA all-star selections, you'd be hard-pressed to label anyone other than Michael Jordan as the GOAT (greatest of all time). Yet Jordan's teammates have often described him as selfish, hostile, and abrasive. Believing that others should play at his elite level, Jordan employed a "school of hard knocks" mentality and regularly yelled at teammates, berated them, and even got into scuffles. Jordan personified an almost militaristic, top-down command-and-control leadership style that subdued players into supporting roles, feeding plays to himself. It's a style that simply wouldn't fly in today's league.

As exceptional a player as Jordan was, the real driving force behind the Chicago Bulls' greatness didn't score a single point and wasn't even a player on the team. Standing on the sidelines was the true leader of the Bulls: coach Phil Jackson. His coaching enabled the team to earn back-to-back "three-peat" victories between 1991 and 1998, cementing the Chicago Bulls as an NBA dynasty. And then he did it all over again: He built another NBA dynasty with Kobe Bryant and the Los Angeles Lakers. From 2002 to 2010, Jackson coached the dysfunctional team to a whopping five NBA Championship victories.

How did he do it? The answer lies deep in Jackson's book, *Eleven Rings: The Soul of Success*, in which Jackson ruminates on the mindset that formed the bedrock of his success. In the book, Jackson lists several principles, most of which derive from practices inspired by his obsession with ancient Buddhist, Zen, and Native American philosophies. Many of his principles, such as "Forget the Ring," "The Key to Success Is Compassion," and especially "Bench the Ego," are centered around the idea of servant leadership—a concept with origins in ancient religions. The modern and refined version of the concept was first articulated by Robert K. Greenleaf in his 1970 essay "The Servant as Leader." As the founder of the modern servant leadership movement, Greenleaf described the servant leader as "servant first"—someone who makes sure that other people's highest-priority needs are being met.

Servant leaders typically have eight key characteristics, according to a Rotterdam School of Management study of more than 1,500 leaders:

1. **Empowerment:** Assisting others in realizing their full potential.

2. **Accountability:** Holding themselves responsible for their actions.

3. **Enabling:** Putting others before themselves.

4. **Humility and self-awareness:** Admitting errors and asking for assistance.

5. **Authenticity:** Being true to oneself.

6. **Courage:** Driving innovation by taking risks and overcoming adversity.

7. **Empathy and healing:** Understanding the perspectives and experiences of others.

8. **Stewardship:** Taking responsibility for the common interest of others.

These leaders are profoundly human-centric and "lead from behind"—a concept integral to the future of work. This type of leader practices servitude, shares the power, puts the needs of others first, and helps people grow and perform at their peak. If you take care of your team, your team will take care of your customers, and your customers will take care of the profits. In this way, giving more gets you more.

Starbucks Corporation understands this better than most organizations. Servant leadership is deeply embedded in the company's culture, among both its corporate and team leaders. At all levels, employee growth is a high priority, as championed by former president Howard Behar, who believed that "employees who are cared for are the ones who care about customers." This is a notion also embraced by Arne Sorenson, CEO of Marriott International, who continuously advocates for safer and more inclusive workplaces.

Following my internship at Sony Music Entertainment, I joined the University of Toronto Scarborough's Department of Student Life as a graphic designer. The first directive I received from my supervisor, Allan Grant, on my very first day of work, perplexed me to no end. He told me to "write yourself out of this job."

To lead with servitude is to make yourself obsolete. But this concept of "writing yourself out of the job" is not the same as making yourself useless. Quite the opposite—it's about being great at what you do, creating a system, planning for succession, training others thoroughly, and delegating generously. If executed successfully, you'll build a solid foundation that will allow you to step up to the next challenge while someone else continues what you started.

Like Jackson did for his players, Grant gave my team meaningful, boundary-pushing projects, as well as the training and mentorship necessary to get them done. He had us thinking about building good habits, which we then translated into systems and processes. And as we developed mastery, we helped others do the same. This freed up our time and empowered us to take on subsequently more significant challenges. That meant that if a leader left the organization altogether, their impact and model would remain.

It's this approach to servant leadership—helping others grow, creating more leaders, and building a system—that I've continued to replicate throughout my own journey as a leader. But sharing power is easier said than done, especially for new leaders eager to make their mark. It requires a substantial shift in mindset.

Shift Your Mindset, Share the Power

In his book *The Human Side of Enterprise*, esteemed social psychologist and management professor Douglas McGregor outlines two styles of management: authoritarian (theory X) and participative (theory Y).

Theory X leaders assume that workers

- Don't enjoy or like their jobs.

- Must always be directed or they'll avoid responsibility.

- Won't deliver work unless controlled, coerced, or threatened.

- Won't perform unless supervised.

- Lack ambition and need external goals to work.

While theory Y leaders assume that workers

- Can manage themselves.

- Should be involved in decision-making.

- Are intrinsically motivated.

- Feel ownership of their work.

- Possess initiative and require little to no management.

- Regard their work as rewarding and challenging.

- Proactively assess and address problems.

Leaders who subscribe to theory X create a top-down, command-and-control environment. With this approach, authority is seldom delegated, and control remains centralized. This not only stifles growth—it's a point of failure in moments of adversity. One of my good friends and mentors, Drew Dudley, very much subscribed to the opposite approach: theory Y. He engaged, motivated, and empowered his team to the extent that it was capable of running autonomously.

Once, befallen by a medical emergency, Drew had to leave an event completely in the hands of his staff. We had come to depend on Drew as our coach and wondered if we could handle things without him.

To my surprise, the event continued without as much as a blip. All members of the team had clear areas of responsibility and were sufficiently trained and empowered to make decisions. While this may make Drew seem dispensable, the opposite is true: Drew's leadership is the gold standard of servant leadership. He generously distributed power to the team, to the extent that it could function at a high level without him. Drew did what great leaders do: He created more leaders.

There's much to learn from how leaders like Jackson and Dudley breathe the spirit of servitude into their teams by shifting their mindset from theory X to theory Y. To operationalize and maximize the value of servitude, you must seek to elevate the people you serve. This value is all about making your team great by helping them self-actualize and removing barriers to their success.

DISCOVER YOUR TEAM'S STRENGTHS

Most people never reach their full potential—what psychologists call self-actualization. In fact, there's a term for this, "psychopathology of normality," which refers to how less than 1 percent of the adult population functions at that high level. And yet it's something we all aspire to.

When a leader helps their team become the best versions of themselves, the investment will pay for itself in the long run. Research by Gallup reveals that employee work groups that receive strengths-based development demonstrate up to 15 percent higher employee engagement, up to 29 percent increased profit, and up to 72 percent lower turnover. There's an old business adage in which a CFO asks the CEO, "What if good people leave?" To which the CEO responds, "What if bad people stay?"

Both situations are worrisome. If your organization is a revolving door of talent, it probably means that effective employees aren't sufficiently challenged and motivated. And if you're constantly underperforming, it probably means that ineffective employees are languishing. As it turns out, both situations require helping people become better versions of themselves.

To unlock the potential of a full human gradient by developing your team's capabilities, a good first step is to empower your employees to discover their strengths. A number of resources are available in the marketplace to help. Here are some of my favorite assessment tools:

- StrengthsFinder

- Lumina Spark

- Myers-Briggs Type Indicator

- EQ-i 2.0 Emotional Intelligence Assessment

- VIA Assessment

I've personally used the five assessments listed above; you'll find links to each (and several others) in the Resources section at the end of this book (page 179). Every time one of my employees completed one of these assessments, they reported feeling more capable and confident, and their productivity noticeably improved, too. Best of all, as a team, they began to leverage and complement one another's strengths.

For the best results, try not to make this a one-time exercise. Repeat the assessment annually; find ways to continue the practice, and use the results to continue an ongoing conversation with your team about personal development. Don't be afraid to think outside the box, either—skills that aren't obviously connected to a job description can be tremendously useful. Consider that Phil Jackson had star players like Kobe Bryant and Shaquille O'Neal complete book reports as a way to cultivate curiosity, open-mindedness, and coachability.

> *Help your team maximize their talents and achieve self-actualization through regular strength discovery exercises.*

CREATE PATHWAYS TO PROFESSIONAL DEVELOPMENT

According to the Society for Human Resource Management (SHRM), only one-third of employees are very satisfied with their organization's commitment to professional development (PD). The gap between the importance of professional development to employees, and their lack of satisfaction with it, can lead to turnover; according to the same SHRM survey, 21 percent of employees say a lack of opportunity for advancement is a reason to leave an organization.

Early in my career when I managed student staff, I had the luxury of being older, wiser, and more experienced than my team. Not only did this advantage give weight to my words, but I was in a position where I could be a coach, mentor, and instructor. I was an all-in-one professional development solution for a young student staff.

But that's not always the case. Sometimes your team may include people who are either close to your age or older, or who specialize in areas that you're not familiar with. Your own experiences may not provide you with the tools necessary to help them develop and self-actualize. Enter structured professional development.

Informal mentoring is valuable. But formal, structured professional development training programs not only allow employees to perform better and prepare themselves for positions of greater responsibility, they can also help employers attract top job candidates. Companies who offer structured PD will retain their best workers and identify future leaders. Ongoing professional development is very appealing to the many employees looking to keep their skills relevant in a rapidly changing world.

Management consulting company Robert Half International has identified six upsides of providing your employees with PD opportunities:

1. Collective knowledge increases.

2. Job satisfaction increases.

3. The company becomes more appealing.

4. You attract high-quality candidates.

5. Your retention strategy improves.

6. Succession planning becomes easier.

What does a PD plan look like? There are plenty of components to work with, which means you can craft an individualized plan for each employee:

- **Books:** Create an office library, and even consider creating a book club to foster discussion and shared ideas.

- **Higher education:** Incentivize professional development by subsidizing tuition.

- **Executive courses:** Pressed for time? Short, intensive courses might be a solution.

- **Certifications:** Make progression in the organization contingent upon earning stripes.

- **Professional memberships:** Place your employees in relevant peer groups.

- **Professional conferences:** Immerse your employees in bouts of off-site learning.

- **Speaking opportunities:** Often, the best way to learn is to share knowledge. Encourage your employees to do internal and external speaking engagements such as panels, workshops, and keynotes.

Create a roster of possibilities, and then follow these three practices to operationalize professional development for your team:

1. Assign the creation of a professional development plan to each employee, empowering them to set their own goals, priorities, and timelines.

2. Ensure that the update of their professional development is a standing agenda item during your one-on-one meetings.

3. Routinely encourage staff to share their takeaways from their professional development activities with the rest of the team.

The goal is to create an overall culture of constant professional development and growth. Structured professional development should be part of your leadership practices. From onboarding to offboarding and everything in between, strive to help your team write themselves out of their jobs (and in the process, potentially level up).

Take Action!

Through formal and informal mentorship, education, and skills training, co-create pathways to personal and professional growth for your team.

REMOVE BLOCKERS TO SUCCESS

In a Chinese parable from the third century, an old master teaches a young prince how to rule by repeatedly sending him to the forest with instructions to listen carefully. Unsatisfied with the prince's recollection of obvious sounds, the master keeps sending the prince back. Finally, the prince reveals that he heard "the sound of flowers opening, the sound of the sun warming the earth, and the sound of grass drinking the morning dew."

To which the master smiles and replies, "To hear the unheard is a necessary discipline to be a good ruler. For only when a ruler has learned to listen closely to the hearts of people, hearing their feelings, pains unexpressed, and complaints unspoken, can he . . . meet the true needs of his citizens."

Are you hearing your team's unspoken messages? It's easy for a leader to think they're attuned to their team's needs. Smiling faces on a Zoom call, pleasant email exchanges, and productive brainstorming sessions can lull leaders into a false sense of security. More often than not, leaders haven't built the necessary rapport with their employees, instead adopting a convenient "one-size-fits-all" approach to soliciting feedback.

As a leader, it's critical to know what's getting in the way of your team's success. This is not something that can be easily assumed or gleaned from performance reports. A different, more human approach is required. Like the young prince, you need to keep seeking deeper insight. Fortunately, there are multiple opportunities to identify underlying problems that are blocking your team's success:

During daily stand-up questions. Every morning, ask your staff to share their top three priorities of the day, and at least one blocker.

During one-on-ones. Ask open-ended questions like, "What's getting in the way of you doing your best work?"

During project briefs. As part of kicking off any project, ask the team to think about what might prevent them from doing their best work on this assignment.

In each of these cases, encourage radical candor from your team. If there is anything, and I mean anything, getting in the way of them doing their best work, you need to know. Is the office too cold? Are they not feeling valued by leadership? Are they struggling with a health issue? Do they feel like they don't have sufficient training? Empower your team to point out blockers for you.

Regular, frank conversations with your team are essential to knowing what's preventing them from realizing their full potential. Once you know, get to work removing those obstacles at a structural level. The human gradient is vast, and in most cases, there isn't a one-size-fits-all solution to removing obstacles. Prepare to tailor your approach to different members of the team.

For instance, Phil Jackson had two particularly enigmatic and challenging players on his Bulls and Lakers teams—Dennis Rodman and Ron Artest (aka Metta Sandiford-Artest), respectively. Both paid close attention to Jackson's body language, which Jackson tailored to communicate with each player effectively. For the mercurial Rodman, Jackson subdued his movements. And for the reticent Artest, Jackson reinforced his words with gestures and facial expressions.

Take notes about what's getting in the way of your team's success, and make it a priority to remove these blockers for them.

Take Action!

At multiple touchpoints, empower your team to provide you with feedback regarding obstacles in their path to success. Then work hard to remove those obstacles from their path.

It's Not You, It's Us

The notorious sports commentator Skip Bayless is well-known for his scalding hot takes. In 1999, he penned a column in reaction to the news that the Los Angeles Lakers had just hired former Chicago Bulls head coach Phil Jackson. Bayless argued that without Michael Jordan, Jackson wouldn't see the same success with the Lakers. "The magic-by-association is non-transferable," he wrote. "Jordan made Jackson, not vice versa."

Skip couldn't have been more wrong. The magic transferred just fine. With Jackson in charge, the Lakers won a total of five championships. How did Coach Jackson do it?

In his book *Eleven Rings*, Jackson describes his meticulous process, but hones in on one key point for the Lakers: He had to bench their egos. Success meant that the game had to be less about the individuals and more about the team as a whole. Jackson began by working with each of the players and making them more coachable, then investing in their professional development. He also sought to empower people on the periphery of the on-court action, such as assistants or bench players.

Leadership isn't about you, or any individual member of the team, for that matter. It's about the whole team. It's great that Tim Cook eats lunch with random employees in Apple's cafeteria, but this is a practice that needs to stick to be truly successful in the long run. The next Apple CEO should do it, too, as should other leaders across the organization. Servitude must be hard-coded into the culture of the organization.

By taking care of your people—helping them self-actualize and removing obstacles from their paths—you nurture a reliable, healthy, and well-cared-for workforce: the type of workforce able to provide a level of service to your end users that will yield the wild success you hope for.

The next few exercises will teach you how to further operationalize the value of servitude, so that it's not just your own aspiration, but a fundamental principle baked into company culture.

ENCOURAGE WEEKEND REFLECTIONS

There's no shortage of research substantiating benefits of an effective and engaged team. But what do you do when you've got a highly diverse group? How do you establish common ground when everyone has different personalities, perspectives, and preferences?

The Creative Unit that I assembled at Ryerson University—an in-house marketing agency of sorts—was as diverse as they come. As the weeks progressed, I saw my team's personality differences play out in various ways: The team was quiet in group settings, they didn't interact with each other as much as I expected, and even their professional conversations seemed strained. Something was missing. I didn't feel like I knew my team, and they didn't feel like they knew one another. That's when I instituted a new practice called "Weekend Highlights and Lowlights." This activity is best done on a Monday, while the weekend is still fresh in everyone's minds. Here's how it could work for your team:

- **Highlight:** Ask every member of your team to share at least one highlight from their weekend (e.g., "I built a deck," "I visited my family," "I played video games," etc.).

- **Lowlight:** Ask every member of your team to share at least one lowlight from their weekend (e.g., "I felt stressed," "I argued with my landlord," "I saw a news story that bummed me out," etc.).

It's that simple. Expect the first few weeks of this activity's implementation to yield forced or even sarcastic answers. But stick with it, and have faith that your team members will come to appreciate, and even look forward to, the interaction. This activity invites people to disclose a little more about themselves each week. The effects are slow but powerful: Over time, your team begins to glimpse who their co-workers are as people, and they become invested in one another's stories. Within weeks, your team will tap into what psychologists call the Zeigarnik effect—a psychological phenomenon in which the human mind seeks to complete unfinished tasks, like the story of whether or not somebody's kid's soccer team won their game last Saturday.

Take Action!

> *To help your staff bond, encourage them to share the ups and downs from their past weekends.*

BUILD A KNOWLEDGE CENTER

One of the major projects my team at Ryerson University was responsible for was the creation of a campus-wide knowledge center that would be powered by the Division of Student Affairs. The idea was to invite people from across the campus to share not just their subject matter expertise (research, insights, best practices, etc.) but especially their individual stories.

According to McKinsey research, employees spend 20 percent of their time at work hunting around for information they need, whether it's in a physical archive, a disorganized email inbox or server, or even the brain of the guy one cubicle over. The purpose of a knowledge center is to consolidate the institutional know-how that's scattered in diverse spaces and make it accessible and searchable for any employee who needs it.

Access to a company-wide knowledge base helps keep employees engaged, which makes them more likely to stay, lowers absenteeism, and produces higher quality work. Productivity goes up, employees feel more included, and they're inspired to contribute their own expertise.

There are more than a few ways you can build a knowledge center (we did almost all of them at Ryerson University):

Create a blog. Invite members from across your organization to contribute articles about themselves, their work, and other topics of interest. New York University's Stern School of

Business published a study in 2011 revealing that blogging in the workplace increases knowledge sharing.

Create an e-newsletter. Regularly email your organization with relevant updates and resources. Search engine optimization platform MOZ does an exceptional job of keeping their users abreast of industry trends through email.

Create a social media community. Centralize online conversations with a hashtag and curate them with a dedicated social media account. Jeep does a great job of even including their customers in the conversation with the help of #jeeplife, #jeepnation, and #jeepfamily.

Invest in a communication platform. Stay aligned as a team and make quicker decisions by centralizing all of your work communication in one easily accessible place. Brands from TD Ameritrade to Electronic Arts use the wildly popular internal messaging platform Slack.

Host a podcast. Podcasts offer a portable and convenient way to produce and deliver content, and to build ongoing relationships with your clients, employees, and stakeholders. David Allen's *Getting Things Done* podcast is an excellent example of this.

Run events. Shopify's Toronto office has become a fixture in the city's creative and business scene. In any given week, it plays host to meetups, panels, hackathons, and more. Shopify employees are given priority access to these diverse community-driven events.

Launch a podcast, newsletter, publication, social media takeover, or a speaker series—something that allows your employees to share know-how and self-actualize. These outlets not only support your team but can also serve as ways to raise the organization's profile and awareness—a win-win.

> *For the benefit of easy access and communication, produce a hub where insights, updates, and best practices can be shared by and across your organization.*

CO-CREATE THE ORGANIZATION

"Think like an owner" is a phrase used by leaders to get their followers to perform at an elite level. But it's a cop-out if the leader doesn't actually *treat* the employee as an owner.

I often find myself thinking back to the first corporate retreat I ever attended, while working at the University of Toronto Scarborough. During that weekend, Liza Arnason (director of Student Life at that time) sat back and empowered her team to dream up the organization they wanted to create. And when we returned to campus, she enabled us to execute those ideas.

She treated us like partners, co-creators in renewing the organization. If you truly want your employees to think like owners, you need to start treating them that way. Here are some practical ways to accomplish this:

Be transparent about how you make business and compensation decisions. When leaders share company goals, focuses, initiatives, and challenges, employees can make better choices regarding their priorities.

Ask employees to set their own goals. The familiar Objectives and Key Results (OKR) method, which dates back to the 1980s, is particularly useful here. It's a simple goal-setting methodology designed to push your team toward your biggest goals and help you monitor your progress in reaching them. It removes misunderstandings and puts responsibility on everyone to meet their commitments. (See the Resources section on page 181 for a guide on how to use OKRs.)

Provide an upside. Give people a stake in the success of the organization. Traditionally, this could be stock options, a monthly bonus, or profit-sharing.

Give stretch assignments. A stretch assignment is a project that requires new expertise to complete. Research from the organizational consulting firm Korn Ferry found that stretch assignments are better than action learning, mentoring, exposure to more senior leaders, and formal classroom training for building skills.

Encourage employee feedback. Regularly ask your employees questions like: What are we doing well? What do we need to improve? What else is on your mind?

Take employee input seriously. Employees who feel like their opinions make a difference in their organization feel more invested in its success. Also, this practice sets a precedent for a feedback-driven environment, in which every person is growing and improving.

Harvard Business School professor Francesca Gino suggests that empowering employees to think like owners is an antidote to disengagement. And the cost of disengaged employees is startling. In the United States alone, it's estimated to be approximately $550 billion a year. And that's only the direct financial losses. What about the negative influences on culture? Poor customer service? Employee attrition? Lower productivity? All these failings are directly linked to employee disengagement.

In addition to investing employees, Gino argues, fostering ownership mentality increases the likelihood that employees will positively impact others around them. When you take the time to encourage employees to think like owners, they'll grow more productive and effective. Additionally, they'll feel more valued as members of the organization.

> *To get the best results out of your team, foster an environ-ment where they think and feel like owners in the company.*

LEADERSHIP TIP:

How Servitude and Accountability Complement One Another

Leaders who exercise servitude create an environment where employees feel empowered. These leaders help employees self-actualize and remove obstacles from their path to success. At best, employees begin to operate like owners, assuming high levels of accountability. As you've learned throughout this book and will continue to appreciate, modern leaders need to transform an organization from the inside out. It starts with them and their ability to shift their mindset.

For most of their seven years together with the Los Angeles Lakers, Kobe Bryant and Phil Jackson's relationship was strained. And at one point, it had ended altogether. Jackson grappled with finding a balance between team play and Bryant's superior scoring. In one incident, he shouted to the Lakers' general manager, "I won't coach this team next year if [Bryant] is still here. He won't listen to anyone. I've had it with this kid."

Jackson has suggested that his relationship with Bryant had been tenuous ever since Jackson suggested in a 2001 interview that Bryant "sabotaged" his high school games. But this was just a rumor, Jackson would soon find out. What Jackson did next is further evidence of his capacity to renew himself as a leader. Rather than let the problem fester, he benched his own ego; the same thing he was asking of his players. He called Kobe to apologize. And then, at the next team meeting, he apologized once again to Kobe, and then to the team. Finding a new equilibrium grounded in honesty and mutual respect, the Lakers would go on to win three more championships together (for a total of five), cementing themselves forever as a legendary NBA dynasty.

A service state of mind doesn't always come easily. Taking an inside-out approach to transforming an organization starts with modern leaders shifting their mindsets. There are bound to be mistakes and missteps long the way. The way a modern leader handles that is to hold themselves accountable. Vice president of Design at Facebook, Julie Zhuo, said it perfectly: "Own your mistakes and remind your team that you are human, just like everyone else."

"If you want to go fast, go alone. If you want to go far, go together."

— AFRICAN PROVERB

CHAPTER 5

Driving Diversity

The importance of diversity in the future of work cannot be overstated. Our world has been in dire need of this recalibration for a long time. For ages, activists have vociferously demanded more equitable and sustainable outcomes for everyone in our interconnected and interdependent world, not just privileged groups. And at long last, those cries for change are morphing into unstoppable action, driven by the people.

We've already touched on the importance of diversity in chapter 2 (page 27), and I'm confident that you've already internalized its value. But if your organization hasn't yet operationalized it, know that it's not too late.

Consider the 2019 Super Bowl halftime show. The National Football League (NFL) had offered the coveted Super Bowl LIII performance slots to megastars Jay-Z, Rihanna, and Cardi B. Alas, one person was standing in the way of the glorious touchdown of a spectacle that could and should have been: NFL quarterback–turned–political activist Colin Kaepernick.

Three years earlier, the star of the San Francisco 49ers refused to stand during the national anthem during a preseason game and instead opted to take a knee: "I am not going to stand up to show pride in a flag for a country that oppresses Black people and people of color," Kaepernick explained in an interview with the NFL. "To me, this is bigger than football, and it would be selfish on my part to look the other way."

It's hard to imagine a bigger leadership moment. Overrepresented by Black men (roughly 70 percent of NFL players are Black), in a country with an unresolved history of slavery, with a criminal justice system brimming with a disproportionate amount of Black bodies, in a news cycle rife with instances of police brutality against unarmed Black people, the NFL was presented with an opportunity to score big in the fight against anti-Black racism. But as you're likely already familiar, the leadership moment that had been handed to the NFL by Kaepernick's protest was fumbled. Hard.

In the lead-up to Super Bowl LIII, NFL commissioner Roger Goodell turned to his team of mostly white team owners, mostly white executives, and a white halftime show director for suggestions on a headliner. Jay-Z, Rihanna, and Cardi B? All had declined. With Black megastars supporting Kaepernick, the NFL had run out of culturally relevant options. And so, rather than making a powerful statement of solidarity in support of Black America by curating a mythical hip-hop moment, the team chose a tone-deaf alternative: Maroon 5. The media viewed the performance as "the worst halftime show ever."

Following the 2019 Super Bowl halftime show debacle, the NFL did what they should have done in the first place: operationalize and maximize the value of diversity. On August 13, 2019, the NFL announced that it was beginning a partnership with Roc Nation, the entertainment company founded and run by Jay-Z, rapper and mogul. The deal would also give Jay-Z a hand in "Inspire Change," the NFL's new initiative concerning "education and economic advancement, police and community relations, and criminal justice reform," according to the NFL's promotional materials. Roc Nation would ask Goodell to pledge that the league spend $100 million over the next 10 years on social justice outreach and causes. At the time of writing, the NFL has raised its financial commitment to end systemic racism from $100 million to a whopping $250 million. Then, in 2020, against the backdrop of nationwide unrest following the killing of George Floyd, Goodell did something surprising: He released a video in which he apologized for how the NFL had continuously failed to support players' protests over racial injustice and police brutality during the national anthem.

Our world has undeniably shifted, ushering in a long-overdue pro-diversity and inclusion paradigm. In response to the murders of George Floyd, Ahmaud Arbery, Breonna Taylor, and other unarmed Black civilians, Black America's fire of consciousness became a full-blown conflagration in 2020. Women, people of color, the LGBTQIA+ community, and allies from every walk of life had made it clear that the status quo was over. Politicians, nonprofits, and brands from Virgin to Ben & Jerry's, from the NBA to Sesame Street, had all come out in support of Black Lives Matter, making it clear to the world that they are anti-racist and deeply committed to diversity and inclusion.

And let's face it—diversity and inclusion are also good for business. Consider a definitive 2015 McKinsey study of 366 public companies, which found that those in the top quartile for diversity in management were more likely to have better-than-average financial returns; 35 percent more likely if they were ethnically diverse, and 15 percent more likely for gender diversity.

Diversity of people, when properly operationalized, unlocks a diversity of expertise, experiences, and perspectives. And a diversity of expertise, experiences, and perspectives offers a distinct competitive advantage: the increased likelihood that an organization will visualize and realize change before it happens.

When Goodell turned to his team in preparation for the 2019 Super Bowl, he unfortunately found himself surrounded by people who shared his viewpoints. Nothing could change, because nothing *had* changed. Substantive change involved Goodell truly shifting his perspective. For new leaders to thrive in the future of work, they must fundamentally change the way they see the world. Only then can they remove barriers, enable full participation, and unlock the power of the human gradient.

A major upshot of the NFL's pivot toward diversity came in the form of Super Bowl LIV in Miami. With full creative control, Roc Nation curated an unforgettable show centered around unapologetically proud Latinx megastars Jennifer Lopez and Shakira. And just like that, the NFL's Super Bowl halftime show was back to A-list business. More importantly, the show restored a measure of credibility, enriched by a thoughtful female empowerment theme that was heavy on diversity. Goodell's NFL, now aided by Jay-Z (who was inspired by Kaepernick), was finally able to step into the future of work, into a new paradigm in which a lack of diversity and inclusion correlates with eventual failure.

If the anecdotes mentioned above and forthcoming ideas are new to you—if they are jarring and possibly clash with your worldview, don't fear. Like Goodell, consider them carefully, open yourself to the possibility of renewal, and take solace in the words of Martin Luther King Jr.: "The time is always right to do the right thing."

A Diverse Perspective

According to the Center for American Progress, there are several significant ways in which diversity in the workplace influences a company, from driving economic growth to capturing a more substantial share of the consumer market. One of the top reasons is that "diversity fosters a more creative and innovative workforce." As previously mentioned, a diversity of people, when properly operationalized, corresponds directly to a diversity of ideas. And a diversity of ideas increases the likelihood of an organization's reinvention.

In a LinkedIn post titled "VC Isn't Concerned about Diversity. It Should Be," co-chair of the Bill & Melinda Gates Foundation, Melinda Gates, wrote, "The data makes clear that diversity is good for business. Companies across industries are more innovative, more profitable, and less likely to take dangerous risks when women and minorities are more equally represented in their ranks." She goes on to explain that when women and people of color don't have "a seat at the table," there are consequences for the company, for their shareholders, and society at large.

In this section, you'll encounter at least three major examples in which a lack of diversity and inclusion created an unbalanced and unhealthy environment, resulting in irreparable damage. The following exercises illustrate how to properly operationalize the values of diversity and inclusion by fundamentally changing your leadership substructure and making substantive changes to your organization. Let's begin.

LEAVE AN EMPTY CHAIR

A recent Deloitte report that examined about 50 organizations globally (which represents over 1 million employees), described a clear connection between an organization's success and its diversity of thinking. Their research showed that "high-performing teams are both cognitively *and* demographically diverse." And these two features are more often than not reflected in a team's demographic diversity.

And yet, as a leader, it's easier to be casually exclusionary than intentionally inclusive. After all, we tend not to enjoy the stress of having our ideas and perspectives challenged by people with contrarian viewpoints. But as Roger Goodell learned, when decisions are made "about people, without people," they tend to miss the mark. And remember the cringe-worthy PepsiCo commercial starring Kendall Jenner? Reports indicate that all six key people who worked on the ad were white. This provoked a tsunami of backlash on social media for seeming to trivialize Black Lives Matter protests. PepsiCo could have easily avoided this ordeal with a simple question when the project was being discussed: Who's not in the room?

As a new leader responsible for creating teams, informing culture, and guiding projects, you must ask yourself this same question early on in any process: Who's not in the room? When you ask that fundamental question, it will almost always reveal the likelihood of executing a bad idea. Don't have enough people to suggest new ideas and adequately stress-test the viable ones? That's how Blockbuster ended up believing that Netflix wasn't a threat; that's how Kodak ended up believing that digital photography was a fad; and that's how the music industry ended up believing that customers would always buy physical recording media.

What you want is something along the lines of Abraham Lincoln's "Team of Rivals" model—a group of diverse thinkers with varied and sometimes opposing ideas, who are empowered to speak up. Such a configuration will require you, as a leader, to foster a culture safe enough for your team to voice new and, especially, contrarian perspectives. It will require patience as well as humility, and even stoicism. But in return, you'll unlock a broad, vibrant gradient of innovative ideas—the very sort that will help your organization renew itself.

Unlock wild success with a diverse perspective by strategically changing the composition of participants sitting around the table. The next time you find yourself leading a meeting of like-minded individuals, leave one chair empty and ask the team: Who's not in the room? Or do it, if not literally, through a standing agenda item that raises the subject. However you choose to focus on being more intentionally inclusive, you must always come back to this question: Who's not in the room?

> *Assess if the team that is about to make decisions adequately represents the people you serve. When in doubt, remember these words: "Nothing about us, without us."*

EXAMINE AND CHALLENGE UNCONSCIOUS BIAS

In 2016, for the second year in a row, all 20 actors nominated by the Academy of Motion Picture Arts and Sciences were white—an omission that, until then, hadn't happened since 1998. BroadwayBlack.com managing editor April Reign, creator of the #OscarsSoWhite hashtag, took to Twitter in 2016 to revive the conversation about it. How did the Oscars manage to get this wrong not once, but twice? The answer has a lot to do with unconscious bias. Consider that a 2012 *Los Angeles Times* inquiry found that nearly 94 percent of Oscar voters were Caucasian and 77 percent were male, with a median age of 62.

In a TED talk about diversity, Yassmin Abdel-Magied explains, "Unconscious bias is not the same as conscious discrimination.... They're the filters through which we see the world around us." We rely on filters to speed up our decision-making. And when time is short and pressure is high, we can rely on them too much.

The #OscarsSoWhite controversy effectively uncovered a systemic problem rooted in unconscious bias: The Oscar voting pool was biased to overlook Black talent, which in turn made studios less likely to support Black talent, thereby minimizing the chance for Black talent to stand out in the first place. This is the very same problem revealed by Harvard's Implicit Association Test, which demonstrates that 75 percent of people have a preference for white people over Black people when it comes to hiring. When the decision-makers are homogeneous, their unconscious bias keeps diversity away.

But this can be fixed. A Los Angeles–based HR consultancy, Peoplescape, produced a great piece about how to fix unconscious bias. The solutions are all about coming to terms with reality:

Face yourself. Raise your awareness about your own biases. A good place to start is to take the aforementioned Implicit Association Test at the Project Implicit website. It's a brief and easy online test (see the Resources section on page 180 for more information).

Face your board. Enabling diversity in an organization starts at the top. Your board members influence the decisions you make based on their own unconscious biases. Don't be afraid to challenge them. In fact, consider running the previous exercise, Leave an Empty Chair (page 107), as a way to identify any imbalance in what should be a holistic board comprised of diverse perspectives, backgrounds, and experiences.

Face your processes. Review your recruitment and promotion processes. Are they geared toward surrounding you with people who are different from you?

Face your team. Seek out workshops that get at the unwritten cultural rules and how everyday stuff can enable behaviors that we don't want to encourage. (Shameless plug: One of my companies, SkillsCamp, offers training on this subject. We've helped leading companies like PepsiCo, Deloitte, and StackAdapt learn what values and behaviors they want to keep and nurture in their organizations.)

It's not enough to state your commitment to diversity and your opposition to overt racism. To truly change, an organization must make unconscious bias education and training a priority. The result is to open up a new array of possibilities, giving rise to critical and commercial victories such as the *Black Panther* film and Roc Nation's partnership with the NFL. By examining and challenging unconscious bias, by allocating time and money toward it, you make diversity a priority. And an investment in diversity is an investment in your organization's longevity.

Take Action!

> *Privilege is invisible to those who have it. Continually educate yourself and your organization about those who might unintentionally be excluded from full participation.*

PERFORM LEADERSHIP TRIALS

"Brilliant jerks" is the term Netflix CEO Reed Hastings uses to describe high performers with low emotional intelligence. When considering them for leadership opportunities, it's all too easy to be persuaded by their charisma and promise. But know that this is often coming at the expense of better, albeit "invisible," candidates.

Throughout my career, time and again, I've noticed a catch-22 when it comes to new leaders: Management tends to hire leaders with leadership experience. In other words, you're likely to become a leader if you're already a leader. And in the absence of a fair decision-making process, management will select leaders with an array of arbitrarily chosen leadership qualities (skewing in favor of the outdated leadership archetypes that are popular in conventional thinking).

I've heard all the traditional arguments in favor of appointing a new leader: "Clients love him," "She really commands a room," "He's always the first one in, the last one out." On the flip side, I've heard a full array of excuses *not* to appoint a new leader: "She doesn't have the personality for it," "He doesn't like to manage people," or "She is too soft."

The Bollywood movie *Nayak* tells the fictitious story of an ambitious TV reporter who is critical of India's unscrupulous chief minister. During a heated debate on national television, the infuriated chief minister challenges the reporter to do his job for a day. The reporter accepts, and more than rises to the occasion. To me, the movie contains the seed for an idea that can break the catch-22 of leadership: leadership trials.

The purpose of conducting leadership trials is to avoid prematurely counting people out. Not everyone is extroverted, quick-witted, or fiercely competitive for a leadership position. Provide people with leadership opportunities, rather than expecting them to come forward on their own, and you cast a wider net. This can be done in a few ways:

Give someone the ability to coordinate a project. For example: "Hey, Amanda, we think you're the perfect person to coordinate the ambassador program from start to finish. What could you do with a $150,000 budget? Please put together a brief for us to review."

Give someone the ability to change a process. For example: "Hey, Connor, you're the person most familiar with our existing content management system. How would you restructure it to be more efficient? We'd love to see a short presentation from you."

Give someone the ability to manage people. For example: "Hey, Samantha, we're going to assign a dedicated social media intern to you for Q4. Could you put together a list of projects for them, along with some learning outcomes? We think you'd be a great coach/mentor."

Leadership trials don't just help people come out of their shell— they also recognize high performers who are falling through the cracks. They're an antidote for what's called "tall poppy syndrome," a phenomenon in some cultures in which high achievers are criticized for standing out. When you invite people to take on leadership opportunities, rather than expect that they go after them on their own, you can mitigate this effect. This is because the leadership opportunity is offered to them, rather than requiring people to claim that they deserve to be ahead of the pack.

You might find some great leadership potential that would otherwise have gone overlooked. Don't wait—run experiments with new and diverse leaders. Take a chance on them and break free of the catch-22.

Take Action!

Provide your team with opportunities to step up and demonstrate their leadership potential, breaking the catch-22 of "new leaders must have leadership experience."

The Power of Inclusion

Following the 2019 Super Bowl halftime show, the NFL was offered a second chance. And following the original #OscarsSoWhite controversy in 2015, the Academy of Motion Picture Arts and Sciences (AMPAS) was also offered a second chance. Two organizations, both criticized for lack of diversity, needed to move quickly and substantively.

Over at the NFL, Goodell signed a partnership with Jay-Z's Roc Nation. In 2020, the NFL's diverse Super Bowl halftime show was a major success, signaling to America and the world that the NFL was committed to earning the trust of Black America. At the AMPAS, president Cheryl Boone Isaacs announced an initiative to make the Academy twice as diverse by the end of the decade. In 2016, however, Isaacs received a packet from a staff member containing the names of the nominations . . . and once again, all the nominees were white.

What did the NFL do that the Oscars failed to do? Both had diversity problems and made swift commitments to increasing diversity. So, where did their approaches diverge? The answer is inclusion.

Inclusion involves removing barriers to full participation, as well as intentionally involving diverse members of your organization in making critical decisions. In a *Harvard Business Review* article titled "To Retain Employees, Focus on Inclusion—Not Just Diversity," Karen Brown, a diversity and inclusion management consultant, acknowledges that most business leaders understand the "diversity" part of diversity and inclusion; it's inclusion that eludes them. She states that "Creating an environment where people can be who they are" is the real challenge. As a modern leader, you must establish an organizational culture that values the unique talents and perspectives of your diverse workforce.

When diversity is maximized through inclusion, the benefits extend beyond boosting retention. In a report by Salesforce Research titled "The Impact of Equality and Values Driven Business," the authors state that "Companies that actively work to make their cultures more inclusive are better positioned to achieve strong customer loyalty as well as boost employee engagement and productivity."

Here are a few key statistics to support this notion:

- Employees who feel acknowledged at work are approximately five times more likely to feel capable of doing their best work.

- Employees who say their organization practices diversity and inclusion are nearly four times more likely to say that they're proud to work there.

- Employees able to bring their full selves to work are nearly three times more likely to say that they're proud to work there and over four times more likely to feel capable of doing their best work.

Professional services network Deloitte's research division recently concluded that inclusiveness in teams extends beyond "nice-to-have" to essential. Teams with inclusive leaders, they found, are 17 percent more likely to report that they are high performing, 20 percent more likely to say they make better decisions, and 29 percent more likely to report behaving in a more collaborative manner. Additionally, increases in perception of inclusion correlated with a reduction in absenteeism costs. All this is to say, employees who feel included tend to apply themselves more fully at work.

In the future of work, failure to practice inclusivity, and therefore operationalize diversity, is practically a death sentence. Following a period of growth and stagnation, every organization must decide if it will renew or decline. With a diverse team, here are some things you can do as a new leader to make it more likely that you renew.

OVERHAUL YOUR SOCIAL ACTIVITIES

Far from merely exclusionary, your organization's social activities might be actively (but unintentionally) causing harm. There comes a point in the life of many a big, buzzy unicorn when it's time to evolve past being a high-valued start-up. At Uber, this happened when the company finally acknowledged the toxic culture that it had allowed to thrive. It happened at Microsoft, with Steve Ballmer himself admitting they had to grow up. And it happened at WeWork's parent company (which was on the verge of a public offering), where they decided to diversify the all-male board by hiring a female director. (By then, it was too late for WeWork; the damage had already been done.)

As a new leader, at a minimum you need to ensure the physical and mental safety of your team. But in the future of work, you'll have to go beyond that. This means paying careful attention to a common blind spot: social activities. The default group activity of grabbing some after-work drinks simply isn't enough. Often this familiar default is a reflection of a leader's unconscious bias. It's how *they* prefer to socialize. But it can come at the expense of parents, introverts, and people who don't (or can't) drink. And in toxic cultures, it can enable predatory behavior.

The onus is on you, as a leader, to take stock of your team's preferences. Ask them what *they* would like to do, and ensure that everyone feels included. Some alternative social activities for you to consider include the following:

- Art gallery and/or museum visits
- Food tastings
- Painting
- Charity events
- Board games
- Lunch-and-learns
- Volunteer opportunities
- Team meals
- Video games
- Tea or coffee house gatherings
- Escape rooms
- Sporting events
- Movies

I'm sure you know the ancient Golden Rule: Treat people the way you want to be treated. But this rule doesn't hold up in our increasingly diverse world. True equality demands a new model—the Platinum Rule, let's call it: Treat people how *they* wish to be treated.

Even the most well-intentioned social activities can devolve into something antisocial. They might build rapport among a small, homogenous group of people. But therein lies the rub: This almost always comes at the expense of excluding the people you need the most.

Take Action!

Create social activities that include all members of your organization. Consider their unique backgrounds and personalities. Better yet, ask them for ideas.

AUDIT YOUR HR PRACTICES

Multiple studies suggest that we place too much trust in the decisions of people who look like us. The higher the homogeneity of the group, the lower the skepticism of the people who compose it. By contrast, diverse groups are more likely to produce the difficult questions that uncover essential information.

Today, there's little doubt about the value of workplace diversity. For instance, research by McKinsey reveals that U.S. public companies with diverse boards have 95 percent higher returns on equity than those without. Staggering numbers like that are impossible to ignore for companies looking to grow and compete. A question that every leader should ask is, "Who does our organization attract?"

To answer that, it's worth evaluating your organization's end-to-end hiring process; not just once, but on a regular basis. It's as simple as creating a T-chart and labeling one column as "This includes" and the other "This excludes." Then apply those descriptors to analyze an assortment of touch points from initial job posting and emails from HR managers, right through to exit interviews and reference letters. In addition to the content of each step of the process, pay attention to language (tone, style, voice, etc.) and carefully reflect on which type of person you're trying to attract (and why). Also consider what types of people are intentionally and unintentionally barred from full participation in the organization.

If you're unclear about who may or may not be affected by your HR practices, look to the University of Michigan's social identity wheel (see the Resource list, page 181). The model outlines 11 categories of human classification: ethnicity; socioeconomic status; gender; sex; sexual orientation; national origin; first language; physical, emotional, or developmental (dis)ability; age; religious or spiritual affiliation; and race. For each of these categories, consider who your organization is including and excluding.

Leaders from Apple's Tim Cook to Disney's Bob Iger have all pledged to substantively repair their organization's HR promises to drive greater diversity and inclusion—which is the competitive advantage necessary to thrive in tomorrow's world, but is also just the right thing to do.

Take Action!

From onboarding to offboarding, evaluate how your culture and processes might be inadvertently attracting, retaining, and repelling people.

CALL PEOPLE IN

When I was delivering a personal branding workshop for an up-and-coming public speaking platform, Women and Color, I was extra cautious about using inclusive language. And for the most part, I was doing well. As I got to the final slide, I felt compelled to go off-script and give a small pep talk. "You have to believe in yourself," I urged the room of women. "When you step onstage, remind yourself that you are worthy, and you are awesome. You deserve to be on that stage." The workshop ended, and I walked away feeling pleased with my message. As I was packing my laptop, one attendee shared constructive criticism that I will never forget.

She began to tell me that, while she appreciated my well-intentioned sentiment, she felt that more nuance was needed: "For many women, especially women of color, words of affirmation aren't enough. We often struggle with deficit thinking, which stems from systemic challenges. And so, while words of affirmation are great, more work needs to be done." I was grateful for the attendee's criticism, as it opened up a very productive conversation about what it's like to be a burgeoning female speaker in a homogeneous and exclusive industry. What she had done, in effect, was call me in. Her approach was constructive and permanent, without using the Q&A at the end of the presentation or social media to shame me or correct me.

While *calling out* has immense value, it can be counterproductive. *Calling in,* on the other hand, aims to get someone to change their problematic behavior through a teachable moment. The primary difference between calling in and calling out is that calling in is done privately, with compassion. Here's how to do it:

Have the conversation in person. Don't do this over email, text, or phone. This needs to be done face-to-face in each other's presence.

Set the tone for the conversation. Balance any fears or apprehensions you have about this conversation by sharing your hopes for the outcome of.

Focus on behavior. Rearticulate what the person did and speak to how it affected you and others, rather than question their motives or intent. The more feedback you can give, the more the person can grow.

Take the call. Sometimes it'll be you, the leader, who needs to be called in. Give your team both the invitation as well as the vocabulary to do so. It doesn't have to be overly complicated. Simply share *when* you'd prefer to be approached (e.g., the same day as the incident) as well as *how* you'd prefer to be approached (e.g., "Hey, could we chat for a few minutes about something you said in this morning's meeting?").

Calling someone in can be a clunky and often difficult exercise. This can be especially well-suited for colleagues who are open to learning and growing. It's a more gentle (and hopefully more impactful) approach.

Take Action!

Rather than publicly reprimand your team for problematic behavior, instead have private conversations in which you can explain what they did, and then create a path for improvement.

LEADERSHIP TIP:
The Power of Integrity

"When the mob and the press and the whole world tell you to move, your job is to plant yourself like a tree by the river of truth, and tell the whole world: No, you move."

—CAPTAIN AMERICA, *AMAZING SPIDER-MAN #537*

A leader with a deep commitment to doing the right thing for the right reason is genuinely inspirational and can lead by example. But a leader who brings this integrity to the plate through their commitment to diversity can truly make a difference.

Integrity is the quality of being honest and having strong moral principles. It's characterized by moral uprightness.

It's hard not to compare Colin Kaepernick's kneeling to Muhammad Ali's draft dodging. Both were acts of protest, guided by strong moral convictions. "Believe in something," Kaepernick said in a famous Nike ad. "Even if it means sacrificing everything."

Kaepernick hasn't changed his stance since day one. His unwavering commitment to changing the system, though initially polarizing, altered the course of history. His integrity brought people together. He unified them and moved them (Jay-Z included) to action. He inspired others, from Justin Trudeau to Mitt Romney, from Roger Goodell to Drew Brees—and millions of people around the world—to stand in solidarity with the Black Lives Matter movement, fundamentally shifting the conversation.

The modern leader must change the organization from the inside out. As such, they must go beyond merely modeling leadership values—they must live them. It's easy to pretend to value diversity. For instance, during the George Floyd protests, millions of social media accounts (including those run by major businesses and world leaders) posted black squares in solidarity with Black Lives Matter. But how many made substantial changes to their organizations? How many leaders generously donated their wealth to combating anti-Black racism the way that Twitter CEO Jack Dorsey did? How many leaders made room for diverse leaders like Reddit CEO Alexis Ohanian did?

The best way to manifest your leadership values is to live them.

"The future enters into us, in order to transform itself in us, long before it happens."

— RAINER MARIA RILKE
(Poet and novelist)

CHAPTER 6

Sparking Innovation

While researching case studies for this book, I found myself drawn to a short video on YouTube with over 3.4 million views. It's titled "Ballmer Laughs at iPhone" and shows Microsoft CEO Steve Ballmer scoffing at the idea of Steve Jobs's forthcoming innovation, dismissing its threat altogether.

The two-minute-and-twenty-two-second video offers a surreal glimpse into the psyche of a leader who failed to operationalize and maximize the value of innovation. In its modern definition (from *Merriam-Webster*), innovation is "a new idea," including creative thoughts and new imaginations in the form of a device or method. For current leaders, innovation is a critical value. And while it can be operationalized independently, innovation can be maximized only if the other SIDE values of servitude, diversity, and empathy are also operationalized. Consider that even a company as large and innovative as Microsoft once stagnated under imbalanced leadership by neglecting those other principles.

Once, at an all-company meeting, Steve Ballmer grabbed an iPhone out of an employee's hands and placed it on the ground. According to those present, he then pretended to stomp on it in front of thousands of Microsoft workers. This small incident offers insight into a much larger problem at Microsoft between 2000 and 2014: a glaring lack of innovation, which nearly tanked the business. Despite Microsoft's remarkable financial performance during Ballmer's 14-year tenure, the company failed to perform on the 21st century's five most important technology trends to date: search, smartphones, mobile operating systems, media, and cloud computing.

How did Microsoft go from leading the 20th century, possessing over 95 percent of the operating systems on computers (almost all on desktops), to completely missing out on the mobile revolution, owning less than 1 percent of mobile operating systems?

The answer has everything to do with what's known as "the innovator's dilemma." In the highly regarded book of the same name, Harvard professor and businessman Clayton Christensen explained why great companies fail: "The very decision-making and resource allocation processes that are key to the success of established companies are the very processes that reject disruptive technologies." In other words, during times of success, leaders are quick to abandon the practices that brought them success in the first place, such as listening to customers, tracking competitors' actions, and investing resources to improve quality.

In the end, Ballmer reluctantly accepted what everyone around him seemed to already know: The reason Microsoft couldn't adequately respond to the changes in the outside environment is that the inside of the company hadn't changed.

Enter Satya Nadella, who in just five short years would single-handedly refresh Microsoft's innovative spirit, make it more valuable than Apple, reestablish its dominance, and chart a bold course for the future. Where Bill Gates and Steve Ballmer had an aggressive drive for absolute hegemony, Satya Nadella strove for sustainability. He would replace internal politics with teamwork, bureaucracy with innovation. And how exactly did he do all this?

By fundamentally shifting the culture at Microsoft, Nadella clearly understood that the inside environment has to change faster than the outside environment. That rather than laugh at a seemingly innocuous incumbent in the market, the modern leader actively anticipates its arrival and positions the company accordingly.

For all his energy and enthusiasm, Steve Ballmer has very little to show for his tenure as Microsoft CEO. It could be said that perhaps his greatest contribution to Microsoft was priming it for the arrival of Satya Nadella—a man who is no stranger to the importance of calculated risks and reinventions.

With a team that's informed by empathy, supported by servitude, and empowered by diversity, you'll be ready to examine the final component of the modern leader prototype: innovation.

Take Calculated Risks

Peter Drucker once said that the two most important functions of a business are "innovation and marketing." Innovation is especially critical in a knowledge economy like the one our modern world operates under. It drives growth, new products, and new methods of delivering value to customers. According to a 2015 PwC study on global innovation, U.S. companies spend $145 billion on research and development each year. And yet, despite this investment, "Innovation remains a difficult quality to cultivate both in leaders and organizational culture." A 2015 study by the Conference Board found that "innovation" was one of the top two challenges to driving business growth, according to the CEOs surveyed ("human capital" was the other).

Merely throwing money at the problem isn't enough. For example, BlackBerry, Motorola, Nokia, and Microsoft all had years (if not decades) in terms of a head start on Apple and Google when it came to capturing the mobile market. Yet all of them failed spectacularly to do so, despite having relatively bottomless research and development budgets. What was behind those failures? Ineffective leadership devolved those companies' cultures into avoidant, risk-averse mind-sets. These organizations lost the creativity to imagine opportunities, as well as the willpower to pursue them.

After dominating the corporate sector, BlackBerry failed to anticipate that it was the ordinary noncorporate consumer who'd drive the rise of smartphones. Motorola sat back and defended the Razr while competitors were coming out with new, innovative smartphone designs. Internal politics caused Nokia's downfall, and Nokia cannibalized itself, making the company increasingly susceptible to external competitive forces. And Microsoft simply entered the game too late, and failed to compete along the lines of price, speed, or quality. They didn't bring anything new or compelling to the game. BlackBerry, Motorola, Nokia, and Microsoft all fell victim to the active inertia that we discussed in chapter 2 (page 32).

Meanwhile, Apple, under Steve Jobs, was all-in on the future, creating an environment where risks were taken and failure was embraced in the process. As it happened, the inside of Apple was changing faster than the outside world. Why didn't other companies just emulate Apple? Innovation, like creativity, doesn't come easily—but not for the reason you think. Consider a recent McKinsey study, which found that 30 percent of professionals believe that their corporate culture prevents innovation, even though their company has the necessary resources. In other words, lack of innovation does not lead to a lack of innovative thinkers but, instead, a culture that stifles creativity and makes them feel unable to voice their ideas.

Bob Iger, CEO of Disney from 2005 to 2020, knew this all too well. At the start of his tenure, when he asked his team to provide him with financial performance reports of the previous decade's slate of animated films, the results were appalling. By failing to produce successful franchises, Disney was losing market share to Pixar, DreamWorks, and other competitors. Thus began a long campaign to reorganize the company, acquire major competitors, and foster a culture of risk-taking (similar to that of Pixar under Ed Catmull). The type of culture that resulted would go on to place big bets on films like *Black Panther* and *Captain Marvel*, as well as on the Disney+ streaming platform, perfectly positioning Disney for the future.

Microsoft and Disney are but two examples of how an organization, no matter its history of success, must substantively change its internal environment to thrive. As a leader, here are some ways to foster a culture conducive to taking bold (but calculated) risks.

LAUNCH A DEDICATED INNOVATION DIVISION

The term "skunk works" originated during World War II when Lockheed Martin siphoned resources into a secret project. Hidden inside a closely guarded circus tent next to an unsuspecting plastics factory was a state-of-the-art incubator in which the first U.S. Army Air Forces jet was being built, the P-80 Shooting Star.

The term has since evolved to describe an innovative, high-priority undertaking involving a small but elite team, outside the standard research and other development channels within an organization (and therefore free from management constraints). Some famous examples of such dedicated innovation divisions include the semi-secret Google X lab, Microsoft Research, special teams at Boeing, and the lab (located behind the Good Earth Restaurant in Cupertino, CA) founded by Steve Jobs to develop the Macintosh computer.

Ready to develop an innovation division for your organization? In their *Harvard Business Review* article "Build an Innovation Engine in 90 Days," strategy consultants Scott Anthony, David Duncan, and Pontus Siren put forth a model for activating a dedicated innovation division:

Day 1–30: Define your innovation buckets. Determine the gap between your organization's growth goals and its current operations. For example, put yourself in Disney CEO Bob Iger's shoes prior to the development of the Disney+ platform. You'd have a growth goal of using technology to reach people in more innovative ways, but you lack the means to do it. Begin your journey by estimating the actual gap between where your organization is today and where it needs to be tomorrow.

Day 20–50: Zero in on a few strategic opportunity areas.
Meet with at least a dozen consumers to probe unmet needs, and then select a handful of opportunity areas. In continuing with the Disney example, would you invest in VR? Well, technology adoption isn't quite there, but it's certainly worth exploring. How about streaming? That's a more realistic option. But Disney content is currently being distributed by streaming juggernaut Netflix. Could you persuade customers to leave Netflix and pay for a proprietary rival service? Unlikely. But what if there was an inexpensive service that customers could purchase in addition to Netflix? Your dedicated innovation department's focus is now clearer.

Day 20–70: Form a small team to develop innovations. Next, dedicate a small group of people to developing innovations. From Bob Iger's vantage point, you'll notice that one of your key partners, BAMTech, is already working on a streaming platform for ESPN. What if you raised your stake in BAMTech and shifted their focus? Better yet, what if you empowered them to become a part of your dedicated innovation team? At this stage, find and eliminate "zombie" innovation projects (those sucking up resources without any real hope of meaningful impact) to keep your skunk works operation even more focused.

Day 45–90: Create a mechanism to shepherd projects. Select and train senior leaders to oversee this dedicated innovation team, and establish oversight rules. Don't treat the development of Disney+ as just another "iron in the fire." It's now a full-blown project. Therefore, add some of your best people to the team and task them with moving it forward. Let the group continue to experiment while you strategically remove obstacles from their path. Further prioritize this project by personally getting involved in conducting the first review of the platform.

The innovator's dilemma seems to present you with two options: play it safe and serve today's customers, or take risks and serve tomorrow's customers. But in his influential book *Built to Last*, author Jim Collins argues that innovative organizations must resist the sort of binary, limited thinking that well-intentioned companies fall victim to. "Highly visionary companies liberate themselves with the 'Genius of the AND,'" Collins writes. "Instead of choosing between A or B, they figure out a way to have both A *and* B." With this approach, you can serve today's customers while also preparing to serve tomorrow's customers.

Disney CEO Bob Iger didn't have to end his deal with Netflix before launching Disney+. By embracing the genius of the "AND," he kept the Netflix deal going while simultaneously developing Disney+. In doing so, he served present customers while preparing to serve future customers.

If you don't have a team dedicated to innovation, consider that in today's world, market share is short-lived. Think about the companies we mentioned earlier, who learned the hard way that to survive, organizations must innovate continuously, coming up with new products and concepts while also attending to their core business and customers.

Steve Jobs once said, "Innovation has nothing to do with how many R&D dollars you have . . . It's not about money. It's about the people you have, how you're led, and how much you get it." With a dedicated innovation division, your organization will continue to tinker and keep one eye firmly fixed on the future.

Take Action!

> Entrust a parallel and insulated team with the task of creating products and services that could theoretically put you out of business. Then get to work building those very things before your competitors do!

ENGINEER CHAOS

While the dedicated innovation division of your organization is busy inventing the future, the rest of your organization should be subjecting its current and planned projects to a stress-testing process known as "chaos engineering."

For example: While supervising Netflix's migration to the cloud in 2011, Greg Orzell set up a tool to simulate extreme dysfunctions in their system. The intent was to drive developers to consider built-in resilience to be an obligation rather than an option. His "Chaos Monkey," Orzell says, is one of Netflix's most effective methods for improving the resilience and quality of their streaming service. It's a program that simulates various points of failure for the streaming platform.

The principle of chaos engineering can be easily adapted from the world of software engineering to any aspect of the organization. Think of it as the discipline of experimenting on the organization, testing its capability to withstand turbulent and unexpected conditions. Rather than wait for the VUCA (volatile, uncertain, complex, and ambiguous) world to afflict your organization, you simulate VUCA characteristics and see how you'd react.

There are two ways to do this:

Anticipate chaos. This comes in the form of a pre-mortem: visualizing a failed endeavor and then reverse-engineering the circumstances of its failure. Doing so will help your organization navigate the future more strategically.

Simulate chaos. Subject your team to a case study and simulate constraints. This can happen in the form of a scenario-based hackathon (a short competition in which people come together to solve problems) or even a team-building activity like visiting an escape room. (I find this to be quite useful in terms of stress-testing my team's resilience, cooperation, creative thinking, observation, and other skills needed during a crisis.)

The goal of any chaos engineering exercise is to run through failure before it happens. Modern leadership, then, is about creative destruction. It is about establishing a need for change when it might not yet be apparent to everyone.

Take Action!

> *Simulate tomorrow's problems today. Learn from your reactions, assess shortcomings, and then prepare for the real thing.*

ASSIGN THE TIME FOR INNOVATION

While a dedicated innovation division and routine chaos engineering are effective, for innovation to truly become a part of the culture, it must be reflected in the organization's budget. Not just its financial budget, but also in the budget that represents the organization's priorities most accurately: time.

Broadly speaking, there are two approaches to this (and they're not mutually exclusive):

Structured time. One of Google's best-known innovation mechanisms was its policy of "20 percent time," allowing engineers to spend 20 percent of their work time on personal projects of their own choosing. The result? Gmail, AdSense, Google Talk, and other popular services. Several top companies, including those in the Fortune 50, use the 70-20-10 model: People spend 70 percent of their time focusing on their main roles, 20 percent on initiatives for the greater good, and 10 percent for learning.

Structured events. Microsoft, under Satya Nadella, hosts the annual Microsoft Hackathon, which the company calls the "largest private hackathon in the world." Though only a handful of the projects pitched lead to mainstream products, any of them could be a game-changing idea one day. Nadella knows that tomorrow is just around the corner.

Allocating an entire organization's time and other resources toward innovation can seem counterproductive. Why, after all, should leaders shift the status quo, especially if there's no revenue to be generated immediately?

Innovation is about generating ideas that will prevent the company from failing in the future. Consider research by the BCG Henderson Institute, which shows that in recessions and downturns, 14 percent of companies outperform both historically and competitively because they invest in new growth areas.

If you can keep your team's imagination alive, especially under pressure, your organization can reap significant value.

Take Action!

Allocate time for your team to follow their own creativity wherever it leads. And allocate financial resources to support experimentation and creative events.

Identify Problems, Offer Solutions

In 2011, Kimberly Bryant enrolled her tech-savvy 10-year-old daughter in the iD Tech camp at Stanford University. To Bryant's dismay, the class was very imbalanced. Of the nearly 40 students, only a handful were girls. And to make matters worse, her daughter was the only person of color. Bryant immediately saw a problem that needed to be solved. She ran her idea of a more balanced program by a few friends, borrowed some money, and ran a pilot. Soon Black Girls Code was born. Since then, Black Girls Code has taught over 14,000 girls across America as well as internationally.

On the other side of the country, while on the election trail for the 2010 Democratic primary, Reshma Saujani discovered the connection between the gender gap in computer sciences and the messages kids received starting at a young age. As reported on MyFounderStory.com, she noticed: "Boys were commended for being brave and taking risks, while girls were encouraged to strive for perfection." Two years later, Reshma launched Girls Who Code, which provides girls aged 3 to 12 with opportunities to learn computer coding in a friendly, girls-only setting.

Saujani and Bryant exemplify the innovative spirit that modern leaders must strive to cultivate in their team. It's one that was taught to me by an early mentor, Glen Weppler. As a new leader, I remember going into Weppler's office at the beginning of my role and laying out several difficulties that I was running into. He observed that my thought process was chaotic and that I was paralyzed by problems. Instead of solving my problems for me, he encouraged me to reflect on these challenges beforehand, rather than dump them on his desk, and present him with solutions. Over several one-on-ones, I rewired my approach to innovation with a more "solutionist" way of thinking.

As a modern leader, it's imperative that you create a culture where problems are not only identified, but are presented along with possible solutions. It's a simple but incredibly useful switch. By creating a solution-focused culture, your organization will remain vigilant and ready to spring into action.

GET REAL ABOUT COMPETITION

In an interview with CNBC, Disney CEO Bob Iger said he's not too concerned about Disney+ competitors. "We're very, very different than any other service that is out there," he said.

Undoubtedly, Netflix and Amazon view Disney+ as competition, just as much as Disney+ views them as competition. After all, Bob Iger didn't become the leader of one of the top 10 media conglomerates in the world without being ruthlessly competitive. Iger's public downplaying of his competitors is reminiscent of a competitive strategy from Sun Tzu's *The Art of War*: "When we are near, we must make the enemy believe we are far away; when far away, we must make him believe we are near."

When considering your competition, it's important to remember that organizations usually have two types:

Direct competitors: Organizations that sell or market the same products as you. Imagine you're Nike's athletic shoe division. Your direct competitors would be Adidas, Reebok, Under Armor, and other predominantly athletic wear brands.

Indirect competitors: Organizations that don't sell or market the same products but compete for your customers in tangential ways. Again, imagine that you're running Nike's athletic shoe division. Your indirect competitors would be non-athletic footwear brands such as Crocs, Skechers, and Timberland.

To know who your **direct competitors** are, follow these three steps:

1. **Conduct market research.** Attend industry conferences, browse trade publications, and keep your eyes peeled in general. Additionally, talk to your sales team and find out which competitors come up in the process.

2. **Solicit customer feedback.** Get to know your customers' journey (more on this in the next exercise), including who they were evaluating before deciding on your brand. Ask them who's currently trying to persuade them away from you.

3. **Browse online communities.** Look to social networks such as LinkedIn, Instagram, and Twitter to see which thought leaders and brands are making noise. Additionally, look to Quora, Reddit, and other discussion forums to see what competitors are being talked about.

To know who your **indirect competitors** are, follow these three steps:

1. **Perform keyword research.** Use a search engine optimization analysis tool such as MOZ or SEMrush to discover what businesses are competing for real estate on Google-based keywords that are important to you.

2. **Analyze search results.** Dissect elements of your value proposition and search for them on the internet. Who else shows up in a search that should yield your name? How are they presenting themselves?

3. **Browse paid data.** Conduct similar searches through Google Ads and look to see who is running ads in your space.

And be sure not to make these mistakes:

Not talking to your customers. No matter how well you think you understand them, you must continuously examine your customers' motivations and pain points. You must ask your customers how they view your brand, as well as how they behave in your brand's immediate and tangential ecosystems. This type of in-depth research will reveal more to you about who your actual competitors are.

Ignoring the outside world. Never rely solely on your organization and your industry to tell you who your competitors are.

Defining the competition too narrowly. All too often, organizations fail to accurately assess who the other players are. Organizations tend to look to other organizations like themselves when sizing up the competition. They see who's sponsoring industry conferences, who's getting featured in trade publications, who is expanding into global markets. But this limited thinking leaves you blind to fresh competitors.

In short, get real about your competition before the competition gets real with you.

Take Action!

> *Don't rely on internal assumptions about your competition. Your direct and indirect competitors aren't always who you think they are.*

TRULY KNOW YOUR END USER

One of Henry Ford's most famous sayings is, "If I had asked people what they wanted, they would have said faster horses." While the message is enlightening, much more nuance is needed in today's ever-changing world.

In his book *Hit Refresh*, Satya Nadella recalled how counter-productive Microsoft's corporate retreats had become and how far removed from their customers' day-to-day the executives were. He shook up his first retreat as CEO by making his executives board shuttles to visit and speak with customers. The experiment worked, Nadella points out: "In the ensuing conversations, they worked out how better to work together. Similarly, cross-business teams were tasked with coming up for suggestions for Microsoft's culture and ended up talking late into the night."

Don't wait for permission. Step out of your office, pick up your phone, schedule video chats, and do whatever it takes to meet with your customers. By directly talking with them, you gain unique first-hand information about many things:

Customer goals: What is the user trying to achieve? Let's assume you're charged with introducing a new coffeehouse in Toronto, Canada. In getting to know your user's journey, you'll first need to understand their overarching motivation. In this case, your user might simply be attempting to delightfully boost their productivity.

Activities: What is the user doing in order to accomplish their goals? Once you understand their larger motivation, you'll want to uncover what the user is currently doing to meet their goal. You might find that they currently frequent their neighborhood Starbucks as well as a hole-in-the-wall pressed juice shop near their office. Indirectly, your target user might also be into nature walks and meditation.

Emotions: What is the user feeling as they pursue their goal? Identify potential gain points. While your user might feel invigorated by their Starbucks coffee blend, perhaps they crave more flavors. And while they love their pressed juices, perhaps they wish the bar had more ample seating.

Barriers: What obstacles are in the user's way? Map out the pain points in your user's journey. Maybe they resent the remote workers who take up all the tables at Starbucks. And perhaps they're starting to get frustrated with the long lines at the juice bar.

This is a very, very simple version of a full journey mapping exercise. But with just this handful of data points, you can begin to vividly imagine a solution for your end user: a hybrid coffee shop/juice bar with bold new blends, a self-serve kiosk, ample seating options, plenty of greenery, and a no-laptop rule.

The goal of this undertaking is attunement, which according to Daniel Pink, author of *To Sell Is Human*, is "the capacity to take another's perspective, to understand their interests, and to see the world from their point of view." (Doesn't that sound like empathy, which we discussed back in chapter 3? Good thing you've already built empathy into your team's operating environment.)

The data you collect via your interactions with customers must culminate in a user journey map, which visualizes a typical customer's interactions with your brand or product. You'll find many tools available for this; I've relied on a set by a company called Strategyzer. In a blog post titled "Starting with the Customer" on Strategyzer.com, the company emphasizes two questions that innovators need to answer:

- What are the most critical jobs, pains, and gains of our customers?
- Are any of these important enough that customers would be willing to pay for our products or services?

Here's an overview of the process from start to finish:

1. **Start with "things to get done."** Start sketching out your plan by describing what tasks a specific customer of yours is trying to accomplish.

2. **Add pains and gains.** Describe the obstacles, hurdles, and difficulties your customer experiences, or could experience, before, during, and after getting the job done. Do the same thing for gains: Detail every benefit your customer expects, desires, or would be surprised by.

3. **Describe your products and services.** List all the products and services your value proposition is built around.

4. **Outline how you intend to create value.** Describe how your products and services create value by either killing customer pains or creating customer gains.

At the 2015 Dreamforce conference, Satya Nadella shocked the world when he pulled out an iPhone onstage to demonstrate Microsoft Office mobile apps. Nadella knew his customers weren't using his company's phones. But he also knew that the marketplace left a lot to be desired when it came to business productivity applications. Insights like these can be known only by intimately understanding your customers and their journey.

> *Understand everything you could know about your end user, and then orient your organization's full capabilities toward serving their needs.*

DREAM WITHOUT CONSTRAINTS

When Reshma Saujani's political career vanished, she hit rock bottom and was able to think about her next move without any restraints. Unburdened by the fear of failure, she conjured up the idea for the wildly successful Girls Who Code (page 133).

Traditional brainstorming exercises are often saddled with real-world restrictions such as budget and human resource limitations. And while constraints can breed creativity, they can just as easily dampen it, especially when it comes to ambitious brainstorming. So it's important to ask: What would happen if we set people free from this sort of deficit thinking and encouraged them to revert to a childlike state of wonderment, dreaming without constraints? What would happen if all lights were green, budgets magically renewed, and customers loved our brand? What would we do differently if we weren't afraid to fail?

For brainstorming sessions that require optimal creativity, get your team to leave real-world limits behind and occupy a different headspace by doing the following:

Induce boredom. A 2014 study in the *Journal of Experimental Social Psychology* found that bored people "are more likely to engage in sensation-seeking"—the ideal precondition for creative thinking. In the time leading up to your brainstorming meeting, diminish your team's workload and encourage them to take things slow.

Provide details in advance. Traditional brainstorming simulates constraints and has people think under pressure. But sometimes new and innovative ideas require time and space, so people can shed the parameters they're used to following. Aim to give your team at least a week to consider the problem you're attempting to solve. Allow them sufficient time to reflect and ruminate, so that they come prepared to the brainstorming meeting with ideas.

Shake up the format. Get out of the boardroom, and if possible, get out of the office altogether. Consider an off-site retreat. There, go for walks (a 2014 Stanford study found a direct link between walking and creative thinking). Better yet, go for walks in nature. Introduce different ways to tease out the best ideas from your team—use individual reflection, breakout rooms, and other formats other than simply shouting out ideas.

Remove constraints. This is the most critical piece of the brainstorming exercise—remove all variables that constrain the organization on a day-to-day basis. Engage in thought experiments: Imagine a world without competitors. Imagine a world in which you were flush with financial resources. How would that change things?

Imagine a world of abundance. Imagine a world without the forces of volatility, uncertainty, complexity, and ambiguity pressing upon you. How would your organization act in that world? Unlock breakthrough creativity in your team by creating the ideal conditions for optimal brainstorming. I think you'll be surprised by what they tell you.

Take Action!

Free yourself from the constraints of your organization's internal and external environments. Occasionally brainstorm as though you have all the resources in the world.

LEADERSHIP TIP:
Learning and Sharing Enable Innovation

The effective leaders in this chapter, from Satya Nadella and Kimberly Bryant to Reshma Saujani and Bob Iger, have all built successful organizations that serve today's customers while keeping their eyes firmly fixed on the unmet and unarticulated needs of tomorrow's end users. All these leaders, including Steve Jobs, have benefited in one way or another from becoming lifelong learners and investing in continuous education and professional development. Additionally, they've all been generous with their knowledge and insights, regularly sharing with their teams. Satya and Iger wrote books, while Bryant and Saujani created schools. As the saying goes, "When a leader teaches, many learn."

Whether it's retweeting relevant articles or publishing books and guides, recapping what you learned at a conference or delivering a keynote address—the more you share, the more you increase your team's capacity for innovation.

Don't suffer the innovator's dilemma like Steve Ballmer. In his quest to maximize profitability, he fostered a culture closed off to new ideas and, as a result, missed every major trend in technology. It is possible to serve today's *and* tomorrow's customers simultaneously. All it takes, as a modern leader, is committing to staying open to new ideas and perspectives. And then dissolving those ideas and perspectives into the organization's culture through active sharing. As the adage goes, "The more you give, the more you get."

Satya Nadella argues that innovation is an art, not a science. Drawing on his passion for the sport of cricket, he suggests that while leaders won't always get it right, it's their "batting average" that defines their longevity in the business world. Nadella, Bryant, Saujani, and Iger are not beyond making mistakes. Nor are any of the other new or reinvented leaders covered in this book. But to Nadella's point, success is about improving the likelihood of meeting the leadership moment with confidence. And internal cultures that promote learning, sharing, and tinkering are better prepared for the future of work than those that are closed-minded.

PART 3

THE ROAD AHEAD

*"Yesterday I was clever,
so I wanted to change the
world. Today I am wise,
so I am changing myself."*

— RUMI
(Poet)

CHAPTER 7

Putting
the Pieces Together

The rate of change in our VUCA (volatile, uncertain, complex, and ambiguous) world is unrelenting. To lead an organization in modern times is to contend with a volume and frequency of challenges unlike anything faced by previous generations of leaders. It demands that modern leaders be human-centric, change-friendly, self-disrupting, and values-driven. By operationalizing and maximizing the values you've learned in this book—servitude, innovation, diversity, and empathy (SIDE)—modern leaders can create organizations that change before they're forced to (or before it's too late).

As a reminder: **Servitude** drives your team's personal and professional growth. **Innovation** prepares organizations for the future. **Diversity** empowers your business with the full range of human potential. And **empathy** develops true attunement between you, your team members, your customers, and the public at large. Together, these values enable people and organizations to thrive in the future of work. Avoidant and autocratic leaders entangled in old paradigms, however, are doomed to failure. It's only a matter of time.

In October of 2015, I had the honor of attending the Forbes Under 30 Summit in Philadelphia, Pennsylvania. I watched as Elizabeth Holmes, clad in her signature Steve Jobs–inspired black turtleneck, emerged to raucous applause from the conference attendees. The founder and CEO of Theranos burrowed into a plush armchair, shifting in her seat until she finally settled on an awkward, and seemingly uncomfortable, hunched lean toward her interviewer. As the cheers subsided, so, too, did the young billionaire's beaming smile. Each time the interviewer remarked on the leader's stellar success, she appeared unusually exuberant. Mischievous, even. It brought to my mind the term "duper's delight," which refers to the pleasure of being able to manipulate someone, a pleasure often made visible to others by flashing a smile at an inappropriate moment.

Two weeks later, a scathing article by *Wall Street Journal* reporter John Carreyrou had all but confirmed what I and several other attendees of that the summit suspected: the Elizabeth Holmes we witnessed was a construct—a rehearsed performance, desperately attempting to gloss over the reality of a withering enterprise. Holmes professed that Theranos would usher in "a world in which nobody has to say good-bye too soon." But as fate would have it, the premature deaths in this tragedy of Greek proportions were Holmes's career and company.

In 1969, Elisabeth Kübler-Ross published *On Death and Dying*, in which she explored the titular subjects from a psychiatric perspective. Her work inspired a model known as the Kübler-Ross change curve, more commonly known as the "five stages of grief" (denial, anger, bargaining, depression, and acceptance). The efficacy of the model to explain an individual's reactions to adversity inspired change management specialists such as Martin Orridge to apply the model to organizations of all shapes and sizes. In *Change Leadership: Developing a Change-Adept Organization*, Orridge claims that individuals and organizations experience death and dying in much the same way: beginning with shock and denial.

That's because, researchers say, we tend to think of death as something unfortunate that happens only to other people. "The brain does not accept that death is related to us," said Yair Dor-Ziderman, at Bar-Ilan University in Israel. "We have this primal mechanism that means when the brain gets information that links self to death, something tells us it's not reliable, so we shouldn't believe it."

As our ever-changing world continues to press up against your organization, you'll be faced with multiple leadership moments that will increasingly appear in the form of crises. Suddenly, the hotel industry had to contend with Airbnb; the Department of Justice filed antitrust charges against Microsoft; and, unexpectedly, General Motors approached bankruptcy during the 2008 financial crisis. From formidable competition to obstructive legislation, from economic downturns to shifting consumer behaviors—in the future of work, there's no shortage of hardship lining a leader's road to victory. Inevitably, they'll test your courage as a leader. In line with the Kübler-Ross change curve, they'll shock you, confound you, enrage you, and sadden you.

But they don't have to defeat you. Your organization's ability to adapt to and withstand adversity depends on who you are as a leader long before you encounter difficulty.

With a horribly askew (if not completely broken) moral compass and a grossly mismanaged team, Elizabeth Holmes failed to capitalize on a wide array of leadership moments. Crisis after crisis eroded the facade that had captivated the world, revealing Holmes as a leader unsuited to make the transition into the future of work, no matter how innovative her vision.

Half a globe away from Theranos's San Francisco headquarters, a radically different leadership story was playing out. Jacinda Ardern's operationalization of the contrastingly bright values of SIDE (servitude, innovation, diversity, and empathy) were elevating her to prominence. In October of 2017, while Theranos approached bankruptcy and the U.S. Securities and Exchange Commission prepared charges against Holmes, Ardern became New Zealand's 40th prime minister (and only the third female prime minister).

Becoming a better leader requires becoming a better human being. A leader is responsible for creating not just priorities for their organization, but also informing the culture of the organization. Tethering yourself to the dark triad of narcissism, Machiavellianism, and psychopathy (page 61) may give you glimpses of success, but as a whole, it is an optical illusion. In an article for *Harvard Business Review* titled "Narcissistic Leaders: The Incredible Pros, the Inevitable Cons," global leadership expert Michael Maccoby claims that the dark triad variety of leaders "can self-destruct and lead their organizations terribly astray."

Seasoned executive leader Mike Vacanti echoes this sentiment. In his book *Believership*, he gets to the root of the problem and argues that the path organizations have been on for at least 30 years, in terms of leading people, is neither desirable nor sustainable. Vacanti argues that fear and greed have been prevalent drivers in our organizations for too long, and this has led to a command-and-control approach that not only dehumanizes people, but represents an incredible waste of talent.

The comparison of Holmes and Ardern as leaders is crucial to understanding the bigger picture of modern leadership. At one point in time, both leaders overlapped in terms of their ability to inspire, motivate, and drive change. Both introduced new ideas, grew their respective organizations, and guided the maturity of their organizations. And then, suddenly, their paths diverged. Ardern renewed herself and continued to ascend, while Holmes declined to change and plummeted into oblivion. Emulating her ascetic and choleric role model Steve Jobs, Holmes had optimized her personality for success in a world that no longer existed—a sort of Silicon Valley "Neverland," in which technology wunderkinds and corporate marauders conspired to disrupt industries and hoard the spoils of war. Ardern, on the other hand, strove for equitable and sustainable outcomes extending beyond New Zealand's borders.

Yes, our world is volatile, uncertain, complex, and ambiguous. But it's also delicate, interconnected, collaborative, and full of promise. To "win" as an organization isn't just about dominating a market and creating wealth for you and your team—it's about creating value for yourself, your customers, your shareholders, everyone involved in the business, the environment, and, ultimately, the world. It's about creating a *new* and *better* normal.

To do that, you'll need to harmonize the four values (SIDE) you've learned thus far—and operationalize and maximize them through their respective exercises. Once you activate these values and make them priorities for your team, they will then become a part of your organization's culture. And once they're part of your organization's culture, you will increase the likelihood that your organization will be well-positioned for future success. The bright SIDE values form a congruent alternative to the dark triad. It's a model with virtually no downside, save the significant investment of time and effort.

As a modern leader, it's important to ask yourself the following three questions in order to thrive in the future of work:

What's the big picture?

When I look at myself and my organization, what pieces are missing from that picture?

How do I put those missing pieces in place?

Understanding the Picture

There exists a tragic predicament with many leaders. While they have a bold vision for their organization, and might even have a strong understanding of how the external environment will change at a distant point in the future, they stumble when it comes one or both of these fundamental requirements:

- They lack the necessary values to pilot the organization through adversity.

- They fail to operationalize the values required of a healthy organizational culture.

We've all heard some variation of the notion that change begins within. Mahatma Gandhi is often quoted as saying, "Be the change you wish to see in the world," while Rumi offers, "Yesterday I was clever, so I wanted to change the world. Today I am wise, so I am changing myself." A most interesting variation on this theme of the inside's influence on the outside—one that you'll find relevant to the art of leadership—comes from Steve Jobs: "Design is the fundamental soul of a man-made creation that ends up expressing itself in successive outer layers of the product or service."

Jobs was referring to the iMac when he riffed on the idea presented above. But his words ring true for the design of an organization as a whole (including its products, services, events, culture, etc.). His description of the "outside" being a manifestation of the "inside" transcends technology products. This concept applies widely to most things, and particularly well to organizational design: The organization is the manifestation of the leader's "fundamental soul," and the leader designs (or at least informs the design of) the organization. Every process, every touchpoint, every product, every aspect of the culture—all of it bears the fingerprints of the leader. Microsoft under Bill Gates's leadership was Bill Gates's Microsoft; Microsoft under Steve Ballmer was Steve Ballmer's Microsoft; Microsoft under Satya Nadella is Satya Nadella's Microsoft. The relationship between the leader and the organization is inextricable.

Having a vision for your organization isn't enough, even if you know how the external environment is going to change. You can't meet the opportunity if you lack the necessary values within you. In the future of work, realizing a bold and brave vision requires a leader with a fundamentally human-centric composition of leadership values, namely the bright SIDE values. Maximizing them will allow you to cross the chasm of time. And the absence of one or more of them creates an imbalanced organization. Let's step back and recall why maximizing these values isn't just a matter of virtue; it's critical for success:

Servitude drives personal and professional growth. When maximized, it helps employees self-actualize and unlocks peak performance. In the absence of servitude, leaders create cultures of conformity that subdue employees into mere conformers.

Innovation prepares the organization for the future. When maximized, it enables people to prepare for their customers' unmet and unarticulated needs long in advance. In the absence of innovation, an organization will fail to transition into the future of work and fall victim to the way things have always been done.

Diversity unlocks human potential. When maximized, it harnesses the collective power of the human gradient: a full range of backgrounds, experiences, and perspectives. In the absence of diversity, an organization will develop blind spots and repeat mistakes. A homogeneous organization remains shackled to the customer base it's always worked with, missing opportunities to grow in a changing world.

Empathy develops an organization's genuine attunement with its internal and external environments. When maximized, it enables a leader to read the pulse of employees, customers, stakeholders, and the general public. In the absence of empathy, a leader becomes oblivious to the realities of their people and the world at large.

Begin your leadership journey by living these values, and you're prepared for the future of work in two ways:

You'll be ready for a crisis. To paraphrase Albert Einstein, "Adversity introduces a person to themselves." A leader's journey is fraught with adversity, and adversity smashes any optical illusions conjured by the leader. How a leader reacts when presented with a difficult leadership moment depends on the training and character you've already established. Therefore, it's in a leader's best interest to maintain a consistent, integrated set of values—one that expects the unknown and that they can trust when the going gets tough.

Scrutiny can't hurt you. Our increasingly VUCA world will strip away any artifice and expose any falsehood around your narrative. Just look at how social media alone, as a sort of reverse-panopticon, has compromised leaders across the board. A careless tweet by CrossFit CEO Greg Glassman cost the company its partnership with Reebok and led him to step down. And following a homophobic comment from its CEO, Chick-fil-A earned a barrage of boycotts and negative press, which damaged the company's reputation. A leader's every word and action is scrutinized under the microscope of change.

To thrive in the future of work, a leader must visualize success at all levels. But what does success look like? In our lifetime, we may very well witness the emergence of "stakeholder capitalism" in which businesses exist not just to maximize profits for shareholders, but to serve the best interests of everyone—employees, customers, the environment, and society at large. It's predicated on an idea that social organizations and capable governments have already figured out: A leader must create value for everyone. And so, when you visualize success, think beyond whatever notions of "victory" you've picked up from old paradigms, especially those of industrial ages long gone.

In the summer of 2019, Business Roundtable—a lobbying organization that represents almost 200 of the world's largest corporations, from Apple to Walmart—proclaimed that the purpose of business now transcends serving shareholders. And the CEO of cloud computing company Salesforce, Marc Benioff, called for a "reinvented system" focused on "employees, customers, communities, and the planet." Some organizations, like Seventh Generation, Patagonia, and Ben & Jerry's, have been championing this approach for years.

True, the majority of business leaders still put the bottom line first. But a tipping point may be upon us. Other leaders are investing in a new leadership template: one that will bring them to the next portal and allow them and their respective organization to step through into a new normal. And they're doing so by operationalizing the bright SIDE values. Because they change themselves, they're able to change their organization's culture. And by changing their organization's culture, they are changing the organization itself. And when the inside of the organization changes faster than the environment outside, it's more prepared to reinvent itself and begin a new upward and forward trajectory over the chasm of time.

This may be the biggest picture: It won't be cruelty or coercion that drives people in the future of work. It won't be merely money and power that will motivate people to build a new and better normal. Are you prepared for this? Is your team?

Find What's Missing

As a modern leader, in addition to understanding the picture, you also have to come to terms with what's keeping you from preparing for it. Which of the bright SIDE values are missing in your organization and yourself?

As an example of what it looks like when all the pieces are in place, consider Jacinda Ardern's 2017 speech to Campaign Launch, which should be mandatory reading for new leaders (you can find a link in the Resources section on page 181). It is the culmination of every major idea we've discussed in this book. In the speech, she clearly articulates a wide range of problems facing her nation. With grit, she rousingly beckons her country to face these problems with the question, "Now what?"

There's much for modern leaders to learn from Ardern. Above all, you can learn that the best way to realize the full power of bright SIDE values is to live them day in and day out. Leadership, in this way, shouldn't begin and end per the workday. Quite the opposite—like the changing environment around you, the values of servitude, innovation, diversity, and empathy must be a consistent part of you.

Perhaps the biggest obstacle to identifying what's missing is that it requires us to accept that we need to make changes. Formulating a better idea of what the world could be is easy. To pursue it, however, is incredibly difficult. It goes against the grain in terms of human nature, for as human beings, we're terrified of the unknown. Hundreds of thousands of years of human evolution have hard-coded in us an aversion to change.

In Greek mythology, the primordial god Khaos emerged at the dawn of creation. He occupied the atmosphere, invisibly and in fog and mist. The name literally meant "chasm" or "gap," referring to the emptiness between the earth and the heavenly space of the gods. The chasm of time, which has been referred to ad nauseam in this book, is something that all leaders fear, whether they admit it or avoid it. The reason is because of the discomfort we're likely to experience as we pass through that gap to what lies beyond. To move from the abstract "earth" to the theoretical "heaven"—to reach your organization's vision of success—means passing through chaos. It requires profound change.

And change is hard. According to Satya Nadella: "It can be painful. The fundamental source of resistance to change is fear of the unknown. Huge questions for which there are no certain answers can be scary."

Like Nadella and the other modern leaders spotlighted in this book, you must invest in your ability to make the unknown known. It's an exercise in contending with information that may oppose your way of thinking and your worldview. It's about facing your fears head-on and searching for answers where you're least willing to look. At first, this practice will destabilize you. Think about how Bob Iger felt when he stepped into the role of CEO and asked to see Disney Animation Studios' abysmal financial performance from the past decade. Then contrast that with how easily Iger was able to shift Disney's entire media business model online with Disney+ toward the end of his career.

As a leader, what you most need to find is often where you're least willing to look.

Once you have a vision of where you want your organization to go, look inward once again. Are you able and willing to change in order to make this journey? And is your team both able and willing to change? If the answer to the first question is no, then success is impossible. And if the answer to the latter question is yes, then success will be difficult (but possible) to attain.

And when you know what's missing, it's time to put those missing pieces in place.

Place the Pieces

In eras past, leaders could survive and even thrive on one or two of the bright SIDE values. For example, Steve Jobs was renowned for being innovative. But Walter Isaacson's biography of the late Apple CEO also revealed him to have tyrannical and coldhearted streaks. This sort of asymmetry doesn't bode well in the present era. As an imbalanced leader, you'll produce an imbalanced organization. And in a world clamoring for balance, your organization will be at a steep disadvantage. This is not to say that your organization should forfeit the competitive advantage of being particularly strong in one quality—just don't rely on it. For as we've seen with Elizabeth Holmes, a single imbalanced virtue (e.g., innovation at any cost) can destroy an entire organization.

If you don't know where to start, I recommend that you follow the exercises in the order in which they appear in this book. I especially recommend this order if you're building or overhauling an organization from the ground up. As you'll visualize in the next chapter, reinvention happens from the inside out. And the order of empathy, servitude, diversity, innovation best mimics this transition. The interlocking values of servitude, innovation, diversity, and empathy must exist together in simultaneous harmony to form a complete bright SIDE value array. The absence of any of them could result in a single point of failure. All the modern leaders described in this book have intentionally or unintentionally been operationalizing and maximizing those values, with the understanding that they would need them when the time came.

As you work on operationalizing and maximizing the bright SIDE values, you'll find that the most effective approach will depend on how desirable one or more values are to your team, and how much resistance there is to making changes.

High desirability and easy to adopt. Nudge your team. Remind them of the benefits of these values, and outline the costs of adoption. For example, Dara Khosrowshahi assured Uber that he would be the opposite of Travis Kalanick, which was welcome news.

High desirability and difficult to adopt. In this scenario, the organization understands why the value is important, but isn't set up to make comprehensive changes very easily. Simplify the process of adopting the value—make it as easy on your team as possible. For example, Satya Nadella had to reduce the sweeping changes he wished to make at Microsoft down to a set of cultural values.

Low desirability and easy to adopt. Once the organization sees the value, they'll be able to execute the needed changes. Seduce your team by highlighting the value's relation to your organization's vision. For example, Jay-Z had to convince Roger

Goodell that entrusting Roc Nation with the NFL's entertainment programming would restore credibility.

Low desirability and difficult to adopt. Start by changing perception. This is perhaps a bigger problem than can be addressed by you alone, so seek allies. Phil Jackson had to overhaul the entire culture of the Los Angeles Lakers, beginning with himself.

Practically speaking, sometimes it's only possible to operationalize one value at a time. Just remember that the absence of traits creates an imbalance, so strive to achieve all of them. For example, if a leader practices servitude, innovation, and diversity, but lacks empathy, this creates a situation in which people aren't felt, heard, or seen. Or let's say innovation is absent. Well, this deprives your organization of the ability to intentionally plan for the future, no matter how well it serves its people and unlocks human potential. All traits must be present, and all traits must be maximized in lockstep.

We are in the midst of what the World Economic Forum describes as "the Great Reset"—an opportunity to rebuild more inclusively and responsibly. History is presenting you with a leadership moment as you read this. Will you seize the moment and help create a more equitable and sustainable society?

A modern leader is human-centric, change-friendly, self-disrupting, and values-driven. They are capable of leading people during relative times of peace, through times of chaos, and back to renewed times of peace. Consider Frodo and the Fellowship of the Ring, in J. R. R. Tolkien's masterwork trilogy *The Lord of the Rings*. Following Joseph Campbell's "Hero's Journey," these characters traversed the path from an ordinary world through an extraordinary world (chaos) back to a new ordinary world. Sounds a bit like a typical organization cycle, doesn't it? Throughout, the characters encountered challenges and adversity, learned lessons, and faced tests in order to ultimately triumph over the greatest challenge of all. And in the end, in a renewed period of peace, they remained prepared for their next call to adventure.

Look past the future of work to the Great Reset, and extrapolate where you will be. In the concerted push at all levels for fairer, more sustainable outcomes supporting the public good, where will you, as a leader, fit? What about your organization?

If you're Roger Goodell when Colin Kaepernick kneels, don't shrug. If you're Steve Ballmer when Steve Jobs unveils the iPhone, don't laugh. If you're Elizabeth Holmes when your soon-to-be whistle-blowers express frustration with your leadership, don't ignore.

Be Tim Cook, prepared to take the reins from Steve Jobs and move forward. Be Justin Trudeau, humble enough to admit your mistakes and earn again the trust of your critics. Be Indra Nooyi, scanning for problems before they snowball.

Prepare yourself today to avoid failure tomorrow. Gain a full picture of the bright SIDE values, assess what's missing from the internal and external environment, and place the missing pieces needed to realize a whole picture.

In the final chapter of this book, you'll gain a model for placing the pieces and for tracking progress. And I hope that it's a model that will guide your organization to endless future success.

It's not an easy model to follow. But it's worth it.

Final Words of Advice

Now what?

I wish I was told at the outset of my leadership journey just how difficult effective leadership would be. Anyone can get promoted. Anyone can start a company. Anyone can hire talent. Anyone can be bestowed with the title of a leader and even appear to be a leader. But what happens when the leadership moments begin to appear? Time and again, you'll have to confront the same question: "Now what?"

And it's ultimately your reaction to that question that influences whether or not your organization will eventually renew itself or decline. With such gravity ascribed to leadership moments, the system of action we call leadership becomes several magnitudes more difficult than what you think it's going to be.

My journey as a new leader was fraught with many obstacles and hardships. I fell down and back during several leadership moments, and I stood out during others. But in the end, what allowed my track record of success to skew positive has been my ability to continually reinvent myself. And that is perhaps the most challenging aspect of leadership: to discard what's working today and forge a model that will work tomorrow.

Organizational change begins from the inside out. It starts with you, the leader. You inform the culture, and the culture, in turn, determines the fate of the organization. Manifesting the bright SIDE values can feel like an insurmountable task. It might seem like the values of servitude, innovation, diversity, and empathy can't be reconciled and balanced by a single person.

But they can. There are hundreds of thousands of modern leaders who are doing it every single day. These are people who know how difficult it is to lead. Still, they choose to do it with integrity and tenacity, and the unwavering belief that exercising servitude, sparking innovation, driving diversity, and practicing empathy is the elixir needed to return to a new normal.

I'm hopeful for a world of modern leaders, guided by bright SIDE values, who recognize that our world is delicate, interconnected, collaborative, and full of promise. And that if we choose to change who we are, that we can refract our inner light to illuminate the road ahead—the road to a brighter future.

"The best way to predict the future is to create it."

— PETER DRUCKER
(Author)

CHAPTER 8

Creating Your Road Map

By reading this book, you've been presented with a leader-ship moment. Maybe you intended to receive one, or perhaps it is coming to you as a surprise. Either way, like most leadership moments, it's here whether you like it or not.

You have what it takes to fashion the values of servi-tude, innovation, diversity, and empathy into the bright SIDE values array that can drive change at scale. It's a model that will allow you to systematically follow in the footsteps of the great and wildly successful leaders profiled in this book.

Reading back-to-back cautionary tales might've even left you feeling fearful. Yes, success is a long road. But rest assured, the payoff is tremendous. Just know that from Nelson Mandela to Howard Schultz, from John F. Kennedy to Ruth Bader Ginsberg, not a single highly regarded leader in history built their legacy overnight. Tim Cook, Dara Khosrowshahi, Jacinda Ardern, and all the other reinvented leaders in this book were, at one point, new leaders transitioning from one paradigm to another, just like you.

Like them, you must tap into the bright SIDE values. And you can fast-track their enhancement with any number of complementary positive attributes. For example, you already know that inclusivity activates diversity. What about attributes such as optimism, advocacy, and awareness? Through optimism, for instance, you can increase your organization's tolerance for adverse experiences. Through advocacy, you can elevate other leaders. And through awareness, you can remain vigilant in shifting environments.

By harnessing the brighter aspects of humanity, a human-centric and change-friendly leader can produce the sort of organization that thrives in adversity. Leadership doesn't have to be a gritty, overly stressful experience. We can retrain our thinking by reframing negative thoughts with positive ones the moment they sneak into our minds. In *The Upside of Stress*, Dr. Kelly McGonigal describes how simply reframing an experience as one that produces eustress ("good stress") instead of distress ("bad stress") is enough to change our response to it physically.

To tie everything together, we're going to learn how to operationalize and maximize the bright SIDE values in a structured way. The goal is to create a resilient, change-ready organization that can adapt to and withstand VUCA forces as it traverses the chasm of time.

Take solace in the idea, especially when the story seems to be at its lowest point, that there is still much narrative to resolve, that your journey is incomplete, and that you've been trusted to lead your organization back to an ordinary world and be further entrusted to repeat the next cycle of renewal. This is it. This is the moment. Now what?

Now it's time to adopt the bright SIDE values in your life. It's time to operationalize and maximize them within your organization. We're on the brink of a new era in thinking and behavior, one that walks a fine line between economic self-interest and the fundamental moral duty to build a good society.

As a new or reinvented leader, you have a massive role to play here. To reinvent your organization, you must reinvent yourself as a leader, and this is far from an easy undertaking. It's a complex and demanding process that requires operationalizing and maximizing the four bright SIDE values through the intentional practice of 24 distinct exercises. As you embark on this journey, you'll want to know where to begin. As you progress through this journey, you'll want to know if you're making progress. And ultimately, you'll want to know if you've succeeded. To reduce the complexity of your campaign, I encourage you to create and maintain a leadership road map. Not a simple, linear road map that charts progress from one point to another; rather, one that respects the scope of the task at hand, as well as your ability to execute several concurrent exercises. Let's get to it.

The Leadership Road Map

With this final tool, you can create a model to visualize the resilient, structurally sound organization you're on the verge of building. You'll be able to see where you've made the most progress, and where you need to shore things up.

To start, take a blank piece of paper (you can also create, or re-create, this road map digitally with the drawing app of your choice). Begin by drawing a horizontal line across the center of the page. Then draw an equal-length vertical line, perpendicular to and passing through the center of the first line, creating a cross or plus shape.

Now you're going to label the four points of your axes, like the points of a compass, with the four SIDE values. At the top of the vertical axis, write the word "Servitude." Moving clockwise, write "Innovation" to the right of the horizontal axis. Continuing clockwise, write the word "Diversity" below the vertical axis. And finally, write the word "Empathy" to the left of the horizontal axis.

Moving along, draw a small diamond at the center of the diagram, where the two lines intersect. This diamond is you, the modern leader—the heart of the organization. You now have four individual pathways that will take you toward the maximum expression of each of the bright SIDE values.

To transform this figure into a model that will guide your growth, divide each of the four paths with six equally spaced notches. Each of those notches represents one of the exercises in this book (recall that there are six exercises in each of the SIDE-focused chapters). Number each of the notches on each path, starting at 1 next to the diamond, with 6 at the notch farthest out. Your diagram should look similar to the one on the facing page.

Here's what your diagram should look like so far:

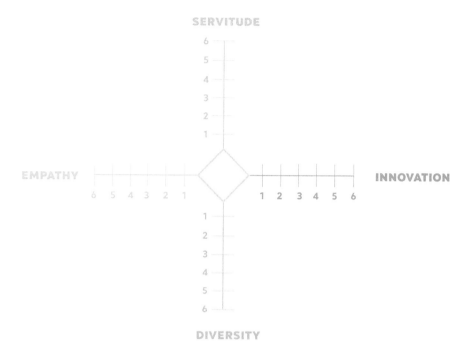

Now take a step back and admire your handiwork. Congratulations! You've created a map showing your journey to becoming a modern leader. And it's also a radar screen, pinging the contours of your organization as a test for balance.

To start using this tool, review the list of exercises on the following page. Then mark a notch on the appropriate path for each one that you've already completed (or that are already part of your operation). For example, if you've done the reverse-engineering exercise, and conducted a listening tour, you'd mark two notches on the empathy path. While the exercises can technically be done in any order, it's my recommendation that you follow the order prescribed in this book.

INNOVATION (CHAPTER 6)

After one month of doing exercises, check your progress by connecting the outermost completed notches to form a quadrilateral shape (see the examples on the following pages). This is what you, as a leader, have manifested so far. Do you have a balanced diamond that covers six notches in all four directions? Probably not, at least at first. Which of the four paths are best represented? Which need more work?

Your goal as a leader is to reach the last notch on each path, creating a "perfect" diamond that reflects a company culture that equally supports the values of servitude, innovation, diversity, and empathy. As you move toward that goal, use this tool to take snapshots along the way so you can make sure your diamond doesn't get too lopsided, indicating one or more virtues have been left unattended.

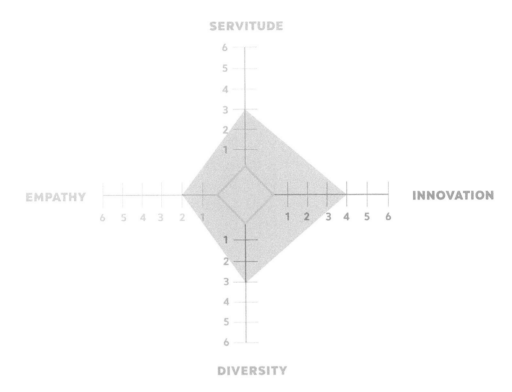

SERVITUDE

EMPATHY — INNOVATION

DIVERSITY

Diamond in the rough:

Work on operationalizing empathy before
your organization becomes too unbalanced.

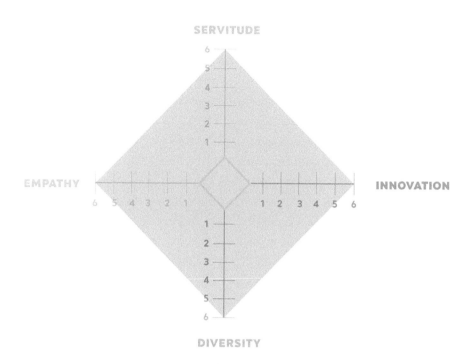

The shape of success:

When all values are maximized, your road map should look like this.

Keep returning to this model as you work toward building a bright and brilliant diamond of an organization. Perfection exists only in diagrams, of course, not reality. But what matters in the end is that you remain in perpetual motion—always vigilant, always changing, always finding new ways to move forward along the bright SIDE paths. Every active leader covered in this book is busy creating an evolving company, preparing doggedly for the next inevitable renewal. A modern leader is always learning and growing. They know that the only constant is constant change.

Ideally, you should review and update the model once a month. You're welcome to do it as frequently as you'd like, but you may find the process discouraging, as you'll be hard-pressed to see substantial progress across smaller intervals. If you aren't able to do it once a month, attempt to do it once a quarter, or at the very least, once or twice a year. Anything less than that, and you risk falling out of practice and missing your mark. Now, it may take you just one year (or less) to fully operationalize and maximize the bright SIDE values, or it may take you several years and then some. Every situation is unique. Do your best, while maintaining a productive sense of urgency.

When a leadership moment appears, it's too late to do anything other than what you've prepared to do. Failure, like success, can be a lagging indicator. The lasting consequences of leadership always happen gradually, then suddenly. And so, from the moment you step into your role or shift your mindset, begin the renewal process. Make sure that at all times, the inside of your organization is changing faster than the outside environment.

Returning to an example from earlier in the book, Jacinda Ardern built upon her success slowly and steadily. Every victory compounded upon the previous victory and built a durable foundation for success—a foundation so resilient and unshakeable that when a 5.8 magnitude earthquake struck in the middle of a televised interview, Ardern barely flinched. Even as the camera visibly shook, Arden, continuing to smile, told the host that "We're just having a bit of an earthquake here . . . quite a decent shake . . ." The host was stunned. Ardern, however, remained composed. When she was asked if she felt safe enough to continue the interview, Ardern happily responded: "(I'm) fine, I'm not under any hanging lights. I look like I'm in a structurally sound place."

Ardern's success was inevitable because Ardern herself—the personification of the bright SIDE values—was undeniable. Just as you are.

In the words of Victor Hugo, "Nothing is more powerful than an idea whose time has come." Here's an idea whose time has come: You can choose to see a crisis as it appears, the way that most leaders see it: an adverse, unexpected, and potentially debilitating experience. Or, you can embrace another perspective and see it as an opportunity to do things differently. To shake things up, rather than be shaken. To disrupt, rather than be disrupted.

Accept that your environment is always in a state of flux, that the future is uncertain, and that it can dramatically change in an instant. And when it does, it's you—a human-centric, change-friendly, self-disrupting, and values-driven leader—who will stand out, while traditional leaders fall back.

In 1917, *Fortune* magazine published its first rankings of the world's largest and most successful companies. But only one company published in that inaugural list still enjoys a position on today's Fortune 500 rankings, more than 100 years later (remember, from page 29?). And that's General Electric.

Why? Because their modern leader, Jack Welch, set a powerful idea into action: **Change before you have to.**

RESOURCES

BOOKS

Leadership: Regional and Global Perspectives by Nuttawuth Muenjohn, et al.
An expansive and accessible academic exploration of leadership.

The Burnout Gamble: Achieve More by Beating Burnout and Building Resilience by Hamza Khan
Written by yours truly, this is a practical guide to learn how to conquer stress and stay motivated.

This Is Day One: A Practical Guide to Leadership That Matters by Drew Dudley
A powerful book that helps people develop their leadership capacity.

COMPETITOR RESEARCH

Here are two robust search engine optimization tools that can provide you with insight into how your competitors are targeting your end users.

- MOZ: MOZ.com
- SEMRush: SEMRush.com

Google Ads
Ads.Google.com
A powerful tool to analyze Google search trends and results, revealing shifts in people's attitudes and behavior.

Quora

Quora.com

An insightful question-and-answer forum that can be used to learn about people's opinions and preferences.

Reddit

Reddit.com

A series of insightful user-driven communities organized around a number of topics of interest.

FILMS AND ONLINE VIDEOS

Downfall, 2004

A riveting movie about the final days of Adolf Hitler's life. Serving as a cautionary tale, it vividly depicts the dark triad and the toxic triangle.

Everyday Leadership

Ted.com/talks/drew_dudley_everyday_leadership?language=en

Commonly referred to as "The Lollipop Moment," this is one of the most popular and inspiring TEDx talks of all time.

Stop Managing, Start Leading

YouTube.com/watch?v=d_HHnEROy_w&feature=youtu.be

My viral TEDx talk about the human-centric future of leadership.

What Does My Headscarf Mean to You?

Ted.com/talks/yassmin_abdel_magied_what_does_my
_headscarf_mean_to_you/transcript?language=en

A moving TEDx talk that illuminates the concept of unconscious bias.

POLICY AND RESEARCH

The United Nations Sustainable Development Goals
UN.org/sustainabledevelopment/sustainable-development-goals/
An array of global priorities agreed upon by numerous world
governments.

The World Economic Forum
WEForum.org
An evolving body of future-focused research informed by business,
political, academic, and other leaders of society.

SERVICES

SkillsCamp
SkillsCamp.co
My soft skills training company, which teaches many of the skills and
values outlined in this book.

STRENGTHS ASSESSMENTS

The following is a collection of eye-opening strengths assessments
that can help you and your team self-actualize, work more intentionally and intelligently, as well as remove blockers to success.

- CliftonStrengths: Gallup.com/cliftonstrengths/en
  /strengthsfinder.aspx

- Lumina Spark: LuminaLearning.com/en_us/products-en_us
  /lumina-spark

- Myers-Briggs Type Indicator: MyersBriggs.org/my-mbti
  -personality-type

- EQ-I 2.0 Emotional Intelligence Assessment:
  EITrainingCompany.com

- VIA Assessments: VIACharacter.org/researchers /assessments

- Everything DiSC: EverythingDiSC.com/Home.aspx

- Leadership Circle Profile: Leadershipcircle.com/en/products /leadership-circle-profile

- Emergenetics: Emergenetics.com

- WorkPlace Big Five Profile: ParadigmPersonality.com/products /workplace-big-five-profile

- Energy Leadership Index Assessment: EnergyLeadership.com /assessment

- TotalSDI: TotalSDI.com

- NeuroColor: NeuroColor.com

- Hogan Assessments: HoganAssessments.com

- PXT Select: PXTSelect.com/Home.aspx

- Core Values Index: ConsciousEndeavors.org/core-values-index

Implicit Association Test

Implicit.Harvard.edu/implicit/takeatest.html
A revealing evaluation of the attitudes and beliefs that people may be unwilling to report.

TOOLS

Manager Tools

Manager-tools.com
A suite of assorted performance management templates for leaders. To this day, I continue to use their one-on-one system.

Objectives and Key Results (OKRs)

Atlassian.com/team-central/project-planning/okrs
A modern and practical guide to the popular goal-setting framework
originally developed by former Intel CEO Andrew Grove.

Social Identity Wheel

Sites.LSA.umich.edu/inclusive-teaching/sample-activities/social
-identity-wheel
A handy model that outlines various intersectionalities. It's especially
helpful when executing the diversity exercises in this book.

Strategyzer

Strategyzer.com
A treasure trove of activities and worksheets essential to the creation
of user personas and user journey maps.

TRANSCRIPT

Jacinda Arden's Speech to Campaign Launch

TheGuardian.com/world/2019/mar/29/jacinda-arderns-speech-at
-christchurch-memorial-full-transcript
This is a must-read for modern leaders. The 40th prime minister of
New Zealand personifies the bright SIDE values in her speech.

REFERENCES

AAUW. "Barriers & Bias: The Status of Women in Leadership." March 2016. AAUW.org/resources/research/barrier-bias.

Abdel-Magied, Yassmin. "Transcript of 'What Does My Headscarf Mean to You?'" TED. Accessed July 28, 2020. Ted.com/talks /yassmin_abdel_magied_what_does_my_headscarf_mean_to_you /transcript?language=en.

Airbnb. "A Message from Co-Founder and CEO Brian Chesky." May 5, 2020. News.Airbnb.com/a-message-from-co-founder-and-ceo -brian-chesky.

Amin, Hiba. "The State of One-on-Ones: Survey Insights from Over 1,000 Managers and Employees." Soapbox. June 19, 2017. SoapboxHQ .com/blog/meetings/one-on-ones.

Anthony, Scott D., David S. Duncan, and Pontus M. A. Siren. "Build an Innovation Engine in 90 Days." *Harvard Business Review*. December 2014. HBR.org/2014/12/build-an-innovation-engine-in-90-days.

Anthony, Scott D., S. Patrick Viguerie, Evan I. Schwartz, and John Van Landeghem. "2018 Corporate Longevity Forecast: Creative Destruction Is Accelerating." InnoSight. Accessed July 23, 2020. InnoSight .com/insight/creative-destruction.

Atlassian Team Central. "Your (Seriously Simple) Guide to OKRs." 2020. Atlassian.com/team-central/project-planning/okrs.

Bacani, Louie. "Lloyd's CEO Receives Damehood." *Insurance Business*. January 4, 2017. InsuranceBusinessMag.com/uk/news /breaking-news/lloyds-ceo-receives-damehood-42225.aspx.

Barsh, Joanna, Marla Capozzi, and Jonathan Davidson. "Leadership and Innovation." *McKinsey Quarterly*. Accessed July 28, 2020. McKinsey.com/business-functions/strategy-and-corporate-finance/our-insights/leadership-and-innovation.

Baumgartner, Natalie. "How to Show Your Workforce That You're Really Listening." *Achievers*. Last modified August 8, 2019. Achievers.com/blog/how-to-show-your-workforce-that-youre-really-listening.

Bayless, Skip. "Jackson Goes West." *Chicago Tribune*. June 17, 1999. ChicagoTribune.com/news/ct-xpm-1999-06-17-9906170098-story.html.

Bennett, Drake, and Nico Grant. "Zoom Goes from Conferencing App to the Pandemic's Social Network." *Bloomberg*. Accessed July 28, 2020. Bloomberg.com/news/features/2020-04-09/zoom-goes-from-conferencing-app-to-the-pandemic-s-social-network.

Bilton, Nick. "Exclusive: How Elizabeth Holmes's House of Cards Came Tumbling Down." *Vanity Fair*. September 6, 2016. VanityFair.com/news/2016/09/elizabeth-holmes-theranos-exclusive.

Bilton, Nick. "'She Never Looks Back': Inside Elizabeth Holmes's Chilling Final Months at Theranos." February 21, 2019. VanityFair.com/news/2019/02/inside-elizabeth-holmess-final-months-at-theranos.

Bouguerra, Sam. "Product Owner — Active Inertia." Medium. November 25, 2017. Medium.com/@bouguerra_70679/product-management-lesson-1-b153ca97aea3.

Bourke, Juliet, and Bernadette Dillon. "The Diversity and Inclusion Revolution: Eight Powerful Truths." *Deloitte Review*, no. 22. January 22, 2018. Deloitte.com/us/en/insights/deloitte-review/issue-22/diversity-and-inclusion-at-work-eight-powerful-truths.html.

Brown, Karen. "To Retain Employees, Focus on Inclusion — Not Just Diversity." *Harvard Business Review*. December 4, 2018. HBR.org/2018/12/to-retain-employees-focus-on-inclusion-not-just-diversity.

Brown, Rachael. Twitter. July 7, 2020. Twitter.com/RCreativeWorld /status/1280392395742490624.

Bughin, Jacques, and Jonathan Woetzel. "Global Trends: Navigating a World of Disruption | McKinsey." McKinsey. Accessed July 28, 2020. McKinsey.com/featured-insights/innovation-and-growth /navigating-a-world-of-disruption.

Burnison, Gary. "Stop Asking 'How Are You?' Harvard Researchers Say This Is What Successful People Do When Making Small Talk." *Make It*. Last modified March 21, 2019. CNBC.com/2019/03/07 /stop-asking-how-are-you-harvard-researchers-say-this-is-how -successful-people-make-small-talk.html.

Carreyrou, John. "Hot Startup Theranos Has Struggled with Its Blood-Test Technology." *Wall Street Journal*. Last modified October 16, 2015. WSJ.com/articles/theranos-has-struggled-with-blood -tests-1444881901.

Catmull, Ed, and Amy Wallace. *Creativity, Inc.: Overcoming the Unseen Forces That Stand in the Way of True Inspiration*. Toronto: Random House, 2014.

CBC News. "'Just Not Ready' Trudeau Ad May Be Getting to Voters, Poll Suggests." Last modified September 6, 2015. CBC.ca/news /politics/conservative-attack-ads-not-ready-justin-trudeau-1.3217203.

Center for Talent Innovation. "Center for Talent Innovation – Research & Insights." TalentInnovation. Accessed July 28, 2020. TalentInnovation.org/publication.cfm?publication=1510.

CEO Today. "1/3rd of Employees Feel Their Company Doesn't Listen to Their Ideas." Last updated August 2, 2018. CEOTodayMagazine.com /2018/08/1-3rd-of-employees-feel-their-company-doesnt-listen-to -their-ideas.

Chainey, Ross. "Jacinda Ardern's Advice for World Leaders: Don't Be on the Wrong Side of History." World Economic Forum. January 22, 2019. WEForum.org/agenda/2019/01/jacinda-ardern.

Chambers, John, and Rik Kirkland. "Cisco's John Chambers on the Digital Era." McKinsey. March 18, 2016. McKinsey.com/industries /technology-media-and-telecommunications/our-insights/ciscos -john-chambers-on-the-digital-era.

Charan, Ram, Jerry Useem, and Ann Harrington. "Why Companies Fail CEOs Offer Every Excuse But the Right One: Their Own Errors. Here Are Ten Mistakes to Avoid." *Fortune*. May 27, 2002. Archive .fortune.com/magazines/fortune/fortune_archive/2002/05/27/323712 /index.htm.

Cheng, Jacqui. "Exclusive: Tim Cook E-Mails Apple Employees: 'Apple Is Not Going to Change.'" Ars Technica. August 25, 2011. ArsTechnica.com/gadgets/2011/08/tim-cook-e-mail-to-apple -employees-apple-is-not-going-to-change.

Christensen, Clayton M. *The Innovator's Dilemma: When New Technologies Cause Great Firms to Fail*. Boston, Mass.: Harvard Business Review Press, 2016.

Chui, Michael, James Manyika, Jacques Bughin, Richard Dobbs, Charles Roxburgh, Hugo Sarrazin, Geoffrey Sands, and Magdalena Westergren. "The Social Economy: Unlocking Value and Productivity through Social Technologies." McKinsey. July 1, 2012. McKinsey.com /industries/technology-media-and-telecommunications/our-insights /the-social-economy.

Ciment, Shoshy. "Nike's New CEO Reveals How the Company Decides When to Take a Stand on Social Issues—and When to Stay Quiet." *Business Insider*. February 9, 2020. Markets.BusinessInsider .com/news/stocks/nike-ceo-john-donahoe-how-company-responds -colin-kaepernick-controversy-2020-2-1028887007#.

Cision PR Newswire. "One Third of Full-Time Workers Globally Say Managing Work-Life Has Become More Difficult—Younger Generations and Parents Hit Hardest." May 5, 2015. PRNewswire .com/news-releases/one-third-of-full-time-workers-globally-say -managing-work-life-has-become-more-difficult----younger -generations-and-parents-hit-hardest-300077259.html.

Cohen, William. "Only Two Basic Organizational Functions: Innovation and Marketing." HR Exchange Network. February 16, 2011. HRExchangeNetwork.com/hr-talent-management/columns /innovation-and-marketing.

Collins, James, and Jerry I. Porras. *Built to Last: Successful Habits of Visionary Companies*. Harper Business, 2004.

Collins, Jim. "Genius of the And." JimCollins.com. Accessed July 26, 2020. JimCollins.com/concepts/genius-of-the-and.html.

Collins, Jim. *Good to Great: Why Some Companies Make the Leap . . . and Others Don't*. New York: Harper Business, 2001.

Collins, Jim and Jerry Porras. *Built to Last: Successful Habits of Visionary Companies*. Harper Business, 1994.

The Conference Board. "CEO Challenge 2015 Research Report." Last modified February 11, 2015. Conference-Board.org/retrievefile .cfm?filename=TCB_1570_15_RR_CEO_Challenge3.pdf&type=subsite.

Dator, James, Sarah Hardy, Caroline Darney, Louis Bien, and Christian D'Andrea. "So Was That the Worst Super Bowl Halftime Show Ever?" SBNation. Last Modified February 4, 2019. SBNation.com /nfl/2019/2/3/18209885/maroon-5-super-bowl-halftime-show -worst-ever.

DDI World. "Global Leadership Forecast 2018." Accessed July 23rd, 2020. https://www.ddiworld.com/research/global-leadershi p-forecast-2018.

Denly, Carla. "LGBT Rights and Protections Are Scarce in Constitutions around the World, UCLA Study Finds." UCLA Newsroom. Accessed July 28, 2020. Newsroom.UCLA.edu/releases/lgbt-rights-and-protections -are-scarce-in-constitutions-around-the-world-ucla-study-finds.

Dierendonck, Dirk van, and Inge Nuijten. "The Servant Leadership Survey: Development and Validation of a Multidimensional Measure." *Journal of Business and Psychology* 26, no. 3 (September 3, 2010): 249–67. DOI.org/10.1007/s10869-010-9194-1.

Doerr, John. *Measure What Matters: OKRs: The Simple Idea that Drives 10x Growth.* New York: Portfolio/Penguin, 2018.

Dubner, Stephen J. "What Does a C.E.O. Actually Do? (Ep. 314) – Freakonomics." *Freakonomics Radio.* January 17, 2018. Freakonomics. com/podcast/c-e-o-actually.

Dwyer, Marge. "Poll Finds a Majority of LGBTQ Americans Report Violence, Threats, or Sexual Harassment Related to Sexual Orientation or Gender Identity; One-Third Report Bathroom Harassment." Harvard.edu. November 21, 2017. HSPH.harvard.edu/news/press -releases/poll-lgbtq-americans-discrimination.

EgonZehnder. "Can Dark Triad Leaders Be a Good Choice for a Leadership Position?" December 7, 2018. EgonZehnder.com/de/insight /can-dark-triad-leaders-be-a-good-choice-for-a-leadership-position.

Etiemble, Frederic. "Starting with the Customer." *Strategyzer* (blog). July 3, 2019. Strategyzer.com/blog/starting-with-the-customer.

Fastenberg, Dan. "'Undercover Boss' CEOs Say What Really Changed after the Show." *Business Insider.* June 10, 2013. BusinessInsider .com/how-undercover-boss-changes-companies-2013-6.

Ferguson, Edward. "Starbucks Corporation's Organizational Culture & Its Characteristics." Panmore Institute. Last modified February 20, 2019. Panmore.com/starbucks-coffee-company-organizational-culture.

Fernández-Aráoz, Claudio. *Great People Decisions: Why They Matter So Much, Why They Are So Hard, and How You Can Master Them.* Audible Studios on Brilliance Audio, 2016.

Fried, Jason, and David Heinemeier Hansson. *Remote: Office Not Required.* New York: Random House, 2013.

Friedman, Uri. "New Zealand's Prime Minister May Be the Most Effective Leader on the Planet." *The Atlantic.* April 19, 2020. TheAtlantic.com/politics/archive/2020/04/jacinda-ardern-new -zealand-leadership-coronavirus/610237.

Gasper, Karen, and Brianna Middlewood. "Approaching Novel Thoughts: Understanding Why Elation and Boredom Promote Associative Thought More Than Distress and Relaxation." *Journal of Experimental Social Psychology* 52 (June 5, 2013), 50–57. DOI.org/10.1016/j.jesp.2013.12.007.

Gallup. "State of the American Manager." Accessed July 30, 2019. Gallup.com/services/182138/state-american-manager.aspx.

Gates, Bill, Nathan Myhrvold, Peter Rinearson, and Donald Domonkos. *The Road Ahead.* Harlow: Pearson Education, 2008.

Gates, Melinda. "VC Isn't Concerned about Diversity. It Should Be." LinkedIn. December 5, 2017. LinkedIn.com/pulse/vc-isnt-concerned -diversity-should-melinda-gates.

Gino, Francesca, and Bradley Staats. "Developing Employees Who Think for Themselves." *Harvard Business Review.* June 3, 2015. HBR.org/2015/06/developing-employees-who-think-for-themselves.

Glassdoor. "Two-Thirds of People Consider Diversity Important When Deciding Where to Work, Glassdoor Survey." November 17, 2014. Glassdoor.com/about-us/twothirds-people-diversity-important -deciding-work-glassdoor-survey-2.

Goleman, Daniel. *Emotional Intelligence: Why It Can Matter More than IQ.* New York: Bantam, 2005.

Greenleaf, Robert K. *The Servant as Leader*. South Orange, NJ: Robert K. Greenleaf Center for Servant Leadership, 2015.

The Guardian. "Jacinda Ardern's Speech at Christchurch Memorial – Full Transcript." March 28, 2019. TheGuardian.com /world/2019/mar/29/jacinda-arderns-speech-at-christchurch -memorial-full-transcript.

Half, Robert. "Professional Development Training: A Win for the Entire Team." Robert Half. February 23, 2017. RobertHalf.com/blog /management-tips/professional-development-training-a-win-for -the-entire-team.

Hewlett, Sylvia Ann, Melinda Marshall, and Laura Sherbin. "How Diversity Can Drive Innovation." *Harvard Business Review*. Accessed July 26, 2020. HBR.org/2013/12/how-diversity-can-drive-innovation.

Hewlett, Sylvia Ann, and Kenji Yoshino. "LGBT-Inclusive Companies Are Better at 3 Big Things." *Harvard Business Review*. February 2, 2016. HBR.org/2016/02/lgbt-inclusive-companies-are-better-at -3-big-things.

Hochschild, Arlie Russell. *Strangers in Their Own Land: Anger and Mourning on the American Right*. New York; London: New Press, 2016.

Horn, John, and Doug Smith. "Movie Academy: Oscar Voters Over-whelmingly White, Male." *Los Angeles Times*. Accessed July 28, 2020. LATimes.com/entertainment/envelope/oscars/la-et-unmasking-oscar -academy-project-html-htmlstory.html.

Hougaard, Rasmus, and Jacqueline Carter. *The Mind of the Leader: How to Lead Yourself, Your People, and Your Organization for Extra-ordinary Results*. Boston, Massachusetts: Harvard Business Review Press, 2018.

Huang, K., M. Yeomans, A. W. Brooks, J. Minson, and F. Gino. "It Doesn't Hurt to Ask: Question-Asking Increases Liking." *Journal of Personality and Social Psychology* 113, no. 3 (September 1, 2017): 430–452. DOI.org/10.1037/pspi0000097.

Hugo, Victor. "A Quote by Victor Hugo." Goodreads.com. Accessed July 28, 2020. Goodreads.com/quotes/381646-nothing-is-more-powerful-than-an-idea-whose-time-has.

Human Rights Campaign. "A Workplace Divided: Understanding the Climate for LGBTQ Workers Nationwide." Accessed July 23, 2020. HRC.org/resources/a-workplace-divided-understanding-the-climate-for-lgbtq-workers-nationwide.

Humby, Michaela. "2018 Will Be the Year of Unconscious Bias." *Peoplescape* (blog). February 22, 2018. PeoplescapeHR.com/2018-will-year-unconscious-bias.

Hunt, Vivian, Dennis Layton, and Sara Prince. "Diversity Matters." McKinsey. February 2, 2015. McKinsey.com/~/media/mckinsey/business%20functions/organization/our%20insights/why%20diversity%20matters/diversity%20matters.pdf.

Iger, Robert. *The Ride of a Lifetime: Lessons Learned from 15 Years as CEO of the Walt Disney Company*. New York: Random House, 2019.

Isaac, Mike. *Super Pumped: The Battle for Uber*. New York: W. W. Norton, 2019.

Isaacson, Walter. *Steve Jobs*. New York: Simon & Schuster, 2011.

Isern, Josep, Mary C. Meaney, and Sarah Wilson. "Corporate Transformation under Pressure." McKinsey. April 1, 2009. McKinsey.com/business-functions/organization/our-insights/corporate-transformation-under-pressure.

Jackson, Peter, dir., *The Lord of the Rings* (film series). 2001–2003; New Line Cinema, 2001–2003. DVD.

Jackson, Phil, and Hugh Delehanty. *Eleven Rings: The Soul of Success*. New York: Penguin Press, 2014.

Jarvis, Rebecca. *The Dropout* (podcast). ABC Audio. 2019. ABCAudio.com/podcasts/the-dropout.

Kahney, Leander. "Why Tim Cook Is a Better Apple CEO than Steve Jobs." Wired UK. April 17, 2019. Wired.co.uk/article/tim-cook-steve-jobs-apple-ceo.

Kerby, Sophia, and Crosby Burns. "The Top 10 Economic Facts of Diversity in the Workplace." Center for American Progress. July 12, 2012. AmericanProgress.org/issues/economy/news/2012/07/12/11900/the-top-10-economic-facts-of-diversity-in-the-workplace.

Khan, Hamza. *The Burnout Gamble: Achieve More by Beating Burnout and Building Resilience*. Toronto: Hamza Khan, 2017.

Khosrowshahi, Dara. "Uber's New Cultural Norms." Uber Newsroom. November 8, 2017. Uber.com/newsroom/ubers-new-cultural-norms.

Kübler-Ross, Elisabeth, and Ira Byock. *On Death & Dying: What the Dying Have to Teach Doctors, Nurses, Clergy & Their Own Families*. New York: Scribner, 2014.

Kuhn, Peter, J., and Marie-Claire Villeval. "Are Women More Attracted to Cooperation Than Men?" The National Bureau of Economic Research. Accessed July 22, 2020. NBER.org/papers/w19277.

Maccoby, Michael. "Narcissistic Leaders: The Incredible Pros, the Inevitable Cons." *Harvard Business Review*. Accessed July 28, 2020. HBR.org/2004/01/narcissistic-leaders-the-incredible-pros-the-inevitable-cons.

Manager Tools. Accessed July 16, 2020. Manager-Tools.com.

Manchester Metropolitan University. "Job Shadowing Guidelines." Accessed July 26, 2020. MMU.ac.uk/media/mmuacuk/content/documents/human-resources/a-z/guidance-procedures-and-handbooks/Job_Shadowing_Guidelines.pdf.

McBride, Jason. "Q&A: Ahmed Ismail, Co-Founder of Hxouse, Wants to Turn Toronto Talents into Global Megastars." *Toronto Life*. November 5, 2019. TorontoLife.com/city/qa-ahmed-ismail-co-founder-of -hxouse-wants-to-turn-toronto-talents-into-global-megastars.

McGonigal, Kelly. *The Upside of Stress: Why Stress Is Good for You, and How to Get Good at It*. New York: Avery, 2016.

McGregor, Douglas, and Joel Cutcher-Gershenfeld. *The Human Side of Enterprise*. New York: McGraw-Hill, 2006.

McIntyre, Catherine. "The Inner Turmoil of Cannabis Tech Company Lift & Co." *The Logic*. May 27, 2019. TheLogic.co/news/the-big-read /the-inner-turmoil-of-cannabis-tech-company-lift-co.

Merriam-Webster, s.v. "Innovation." Accessed July 1, 2020. Merriam-Webster.com/dictionary/innovation.

Mishra, Subodh. "U.S. Board Diversity Trends in 2019." Harvard.edu. June 18, 2019. CorpGov.law.harvard.edu/2019/06/18/u-s-board -diversity-trends-in-2019.

Miller, Jeff. "Bozoma Saint John Explains Why She Left Uber." *Variety*. March 13, 2019. Variety.com/2019/biz/news/bozoma-saint -john-leaving-uber-apple-endeavor-1203162824.

Moore, Allen. "Strategy Activation: Planning a Leadership Development Journey." Korn Ferry. Accessed July 28, 2020. KornFerry .com/insights/articles/strategy-activation-planning-leadership -development-journey.

Muenjohn, Nuttawuth, Adela McMurray, Mario Fernando, James Hunt, Martin Fitzgerald, Bernard McKenna, Ali Intezari, Sarah Bankins, and Jenny Waterhouse. *Leadership: Regional and Global Perspectives*. Cambridge University Press, 2018.

My Founder Story. "WHYography of the Week: Reshma Saujani, Girls Who Code." Accessed July 16, 2020. MyFounderStory.com /whyography-of-the-week-reshma-saujani-girls-who-code.

Newcomer, Eric. "In Video, Uber CEO Argues with Driver Over Falling Fares." *Bloomberg*. February 28, 2017. Bloomberg.com/news /articles/2017-02-28/in-video-uber-ceo-argues-with-driver-over -falling-fares.

NFL. "Colin Kaepernick Explains Why He Sat During National Anthem." August 27, 2016. NFL.com/news/colin-kaepernick -explains-why-he-sat-during-national-anthem-0ap3000000 691077?sp-cl-mc-af-pj=&source=pepperjam&publisherId=96525 &clickId=3195717807.

NFL. "Inspire Change." Last modified 2020. Operations.NFL.com /football-ops/economic-social-impact/inspire-change.

NYU Stern. "Study Shows Long-Term Benefits to Blogging in the Workplace." March 2, 2011. Stern.NYU.edu/experience-stern /news-events/uat_024183.

Orridge, Martin. *Change Leadership: Developing a Change-Adept Organization*. Aldershot, UK: Gower, 2012.

Oster, Shai. "In China, 1,600 People Die Every Day from Working Too Hard." *Bloomberg*. July 3, 2014. Bloomberg.com/news/articles /2014-07-03/in-china-white-collar-workers-are-dying-from-overwork.

Padilla, Art, Robert Hogan, and Robert B. Kaiser. "The Toxic Triangle: Destructive Leaders, Susceptible Followers, and Conducive Environments." *The Leadership Quarterly* 18, no. 3 (June 2007): 176–94. DOI.org/10.1016/j.leaqua.2007.03.001.

Paulhus, Delroy L., and Kevin M. Williams. "The Dark Triad of Personality: Narcissism, Machiavellianism, and Psychopathy." *Journal of Research in Personality* 36, no. 6 (December 2002): 556–63. DOI.org/10.1016/s0092-6566(02)00505-6.

Peisner, David. "How Dara Khosrowshahi's Iranian Heritage Shapes How He Leads Uber." *Fast Company*. October 23, 2018. FastCompany .com/90245381/how-dara-khosrowshahi-iranian-heritage-shapes -how-he-leads-uber.

Pink, Daniel H. *To Sell Is Human: The Surprising Truth About Moving Others*. New York: Riverhead Books, 2013.

Ravikant, Naval. Twitter. Accessed July 28, 2020. Twitter.com/naval /status/1242313978325303296.

Reeves, Martin, David Rhodes, Christian Ketels, and Kevin Whitaker. "Advantage in Adversity: Winning the Next Downturn." BCG Henderson Institute. January 18, 2019. BCGHendersonInstitute.com /advantage-in-adversity-winning-the-next-downturn-5853b4425db1 ?gi=c23323c2f4b9.

Retallick, Alyssa. "The Cost of a Disengaged Employee." Glassdoor. May 25, 2015. Glassdoor.com/employers/blog/the-cost-of-a -disengaged-employee.

Rigoni, Brandon, and Jim Asplund. "Strengths-Based Employee Development: The Business Results." Gallup. July 7, 2016. Gallup .com/workplace/236297/strengths-based-employee-development -business-results.aspx.

Salesforce. "The Impact of Equality and Values Driven Business." Accessed July 28, 2020. Salesforce.com/ca/contents/impact -of-equality.

Sample, Ian. "Doubting Death: How Our Brains Shield Us from Mortal Truth." *The Guardian*. October 19, 2019. TheGuardian.com /science/2019/oct/19/doubting-death-how-our-brains-shield-us -from-mortal-truth.

Sander, Gordon F. "Premier for a Pandemic: How Millennial Sanna Marin Won Finland's Approval." *Christian Science Monitor*. April 6, 2020. CSMonitor.com/World/Europe/2020/0406/Premier-for-a -pandemic-How-millennial-Sanna-Marin-won-Finland-s-approval.

Satya Nadella. 2019. *Hit Refresh: The Quest to Rediscover Microsoft's Soul and Imagine a Better Future for Everyone*. New York: Harper Business, 2017.

Savitz, Eric. "Jack Dorsey: Leadership Secrets of Twitter and Square." *Forbes*. October 17, 2012. Forbes.com/sites/ericsavitz/2012/10/17/jack -dorsey-the-leadership-secrets-of-twitter-and-square/#4a17a4b25e2b.

Schiffer, Zoe. "Emotional Baggage." The Verge. December 5, 2019. TheVerge.com/2019/12/5/20995453/away-luggage-ceo-steph-korey -toxic-work-environment-travel-inclusion.

Schleckser, Jim. "Why Netflix Doesn't Tolerate Brilliant Jerks." *Inc*. February 2, 2016. Inc.com/jim-schleckser/why-netflix-doesn-t -tolerate-brilliant-jerks.html.

Shanmugam, Shankar, dir., *Nayak*. 2001; Soham Rockstar Entertain- ment, 2001. DVD.

Sherbin, Laura, and Ripa Rashid. "Diversity Doesn't Stick Without Inclusion." *Harvard Business Review*. February 01, 2017. HBR.org/2017 /02/diversity-doesnt-stick-without-inclusion.

SHRM. "Making the Case for Professional Development Benefits." Last modified December 20, 2017. SHRM.org/hr-today/trends-and -forecasting/research-and-surveys/pages/2017-employee-benefits -professional-development.aspx.

Smugmacgeek. "Ballmer Laughs at iPhone." Video file, 2:22. YouTube. September 18, 2007. YouTube.com/watch?v=eywi0h_Y5_U&t=18s.

Sorenson, Susan. "How Employee Engagement Drives Growth." Gallup. June 20, 2013. Gallup.com/workplace/236927/employee -engagement-drives-growth.aspx.

Stanford Graduate School of Business. "The Challenge of Change in Business." Facebook. Accessed July 28, 2020. Facebook.com /StanfordGSB/videos/699286793899263.

Stankiewicz, Kevin. "Disney is 'not fixated' on lower price of Apple's streaming service, CEO Bob Iger says." CNBC. October 22, 2019. CNBC.com/2019/10/22/ceo-bob-iger-disney-not-fixated-on-cost-of -apples-streaming-service.html.

Star Staff. "Transcript of Trudeau's Responses to Reporters Addressing 2001 Brownface Photo." *The Star.* September 18, 2019. TheStar.com/politics/federal/2019/09/18/transcript-of-trudeaus-responses-to-reporters-addressing-2001-brownface-photo.html.

Straczynski, J. Michael. *Amazing Spider-Man #537.* Marvel, 2007.

Sull, Donald. "Why Good Companies Go Bad." *Harvard Business Review.* Accessed July 28, 2020. HBR.org/1999/07/why-good-companies-go-bad.

Tabaka, Marla. "5 Leadership Lessons from Twitter CEO Jack Dorsey." *Inc.* September 2, 2015. Inc.com/marla-tabaka/5-things-jack-dorsey-s-style-can-teach-you-about-being-a-better-leader.html.

TransEquality. "The Report of the 2015 U.S. Transgender Survey." Accessed July 28, 2020. TransEquality.org/sites/default/files/docs/usts/USTS-Executive-Summary-Dec17.pdf.

Tucker, Rebecca. "Coronavirus: This Is How We Get Laid Off Now, at Home, Alone." *Vice.* March 24, 2020. Vice.com/en_us/article/xgqpa7/this-is-how-we-get-laid-off-now-at-home-alone.

Turban, Stephen, Dan Wu, and Letian Zhang. "Research: When Gender Diversity Makes Firms More Productive." *Harvard Business Review.* February 11, 2019. HBR.org/2019/02/research-when-gender-diversity-makes-firms-more-productive.

Tzu, Sun. *The Art of War.* Pretorian Books, 2020.

University of Michigan. "Social Identity Wheel." Accessed July 28, 2020. Sites.LSA.umich.edu/inclusive-teaching/sample-activities/social-identity-wheel.

Vacanti, Mike. *Believership: The Superpower Beyond Leadership: Volume 1, The Experience.* Dog Ear Publishing, 2019.

Vlaskovits, Patrick. "Henry Ford, Innovation, and That 'Faster Horse' Quote." *Harvard Business Review.* August 29, 2011. HBR.org/2011/08/henry-ford-never-said-the-fast.

Wiener-Bronner, Danielle. "How Indra Nooyi Built Pepsi for the Future." CNN Business. August 7, 2018. Money.CNN.com/2018/08/07/news/companies/indra-nooyi-legacy.

Weiner, Yitzi. "The Inspiring Backstory of Eric S. Yuan, Founder and CEO of Zoom." *Medium*. October 2, 2017. Medium.com/thrive-global/the-inspiring-backstory-of-eric-s-yuan-founder-and-ceo-of-zoom-98b7fab8cacc.

Willink, Jocko, and Leif Babin. *Extreme Ownership: How U.S. Navy SEALs Lead and Win*. New York: St. Martin's Press, 2015.

Willink, Jocko, and Leif Babin. *The Dichotomy of Leadership*. Sydney Pan Macmillan Australia, 2018.

Wong, May. "Stanford Study Finds Walking Improves Creativity." Stanford News. April 24, 2014. News.Stanford.edu/2014/04/24/walking-vs-sitting-042414.

World Bank. "Labor Force Participation Rate, Female (% of Female Population Ages 15+) (Modeled ILO Estimate)." June 21, 2020. Data.WorldBank.org/indicator/SL.TLF.CACT.FE.ZS.

Yates, William B. "The Second Coming." Poetry Foundation. Accessed July 28, 2020. PoetryFoundation.org/poems/43290/the-second-coming.

Yuan, Eric. "A Message to Our Users." *Zoom* (blog). April 1, 2020. Blog.Zoom.us/a-message-to-our-users.

Zhuo, Julie, and Pablo Stanley. *The Making of a Manager: What to Do When Everyone Looks to You*. New York: Portfolio/Penguin, 2019.

INDEX

importance of learning and
    sharing, 141–142
"innovator's dilemma," 124, 141
knowing your competition, 133–136
knowing your end users, 136–139
"solutionist" thinking, 132–133
Steve Ballmer and Microsoft
    example, 123–125
value of, 7–8, 11, 148, 153
Integrity, 120–121
Isaac, Mike, 27
Isaacs, Cheryl Boone, 113
Isaacson, Walter, 157
Ismail, Ahmed, 15–16

J

Jackson, Phil, 82, 84, 86, 87, 92, 93,
    99–100, 159
Jay-Z, 36, 52, 104–106, 113, 120, 158–159
Jeep, 96
Jenner, Kendall, 108
Jenner, Kylie, 52
Jobs, Steve, 6, 23–24, 123, 126, 127, 129, 141,
    152, 157, 160
Job shadowing, 76–78
Jones, Jeff, 27
Jordan, Michael, 80, 82, 93
Jung, Carl, 75

K

Kaepernick, Colin, 36, 50, 104, 106, 120, 160
Kaiser, Robert, 63
Kalanick, Travis, 27–28, 33, 51, 62, 158
Kennedy, John F., 166
Khan, Mehmood, 20–21
Khan, Mustafa, 5
Khosrowshahi, Dara, 53–54, 158, 166
King, Martin Luther, Jr., 81, 106
Knowledge centers, 95–97

Kodak, 108
Korey, Steph, 60–61, 62
Kübler-Ross, Elisabeth, 148

L

Laissez-faire leadership, 35
Law of Accelerating Returns, 36
Leadership
    changing meanings of, 17–19
    LGBTQIA+ community in, 45–50
    modern, 18–19, 159–160
    POC in, 50–54
    road map, 168–175
    styles, 35–36
    in times of adversity, 3–9
    toxic, 61–62, 63–64, 150
    trials, 111–113
    women in, 40–45
Leadership (Hunt), 17–18
Leadership moments, 6
"Lead from behind" concept, 83
LGBTQIA+ community in leadership,
    45–50
Lincoln, Abraham, 108
Listening tours, 67–68
Lockheed Martin, 127
Lopez, Jennifer, 106
Lord of the Rings, The (Tolkien), 159
Lowe's, 50

M

Maccoby, Michael, 150
Machiavellianism, 61
Mandela, Nelson, 166
Marin, Sanna, 44
Maroon 5, 104
Marriott International, 84
Mastercard, 50
McEwan, Aaron, 4

ACKNOWLEDGMENTS

This book would not have been possible without the support of several exceptional individuals.

Firstly, I'd like to thank the many leaders whom I had the privilege to work for and learn from during my career. In one way or another, you've all informed and inspired the insights and practices in this book. Thank you to Mustafa Khan, Altaaf Khan, Sergeant O'Neal, Sergeant Brown, Simon Rayner, Allan Grant, Drew Dudley, Liza Arnason, Peter Scott, Ada Tsang, Andrea Wong, Brad Parry, David Lucatch, Tim Shaw, Lesley D'Souza, Glen Weppler, Bhupesh Shah, Rachel Barreca, Ed Cabellon, Ian Crookshank, Dr. John Austin, Kareem Rahaman, Bailey Parnell, Dr. Kathleen Kerr, Dr. Kathleen Pirrie Adams, Dr. John Shiga, Stephen Sills, Michael Hills, Kimberly Quinlan, Steve Woodall, and T.J. Donnelly.

Next, I'd like to thank the myriad people who trusted me to lead them. I'm afraid there aren't enough pages left to name all of you, but you know who you are. Thank you to my colleagues in the Canadian Armed Forces, NBP Media, UTSC Department of Student Life, EVCN, Rotman School of Management, SCSU, Intertainment Media, Splash Effect, RU Student Life, Seneca SoMe, Year One, 99U: Local, SA Creative Unit, ACPA, SATechTO, SkillsCamp, The Burnout Gamble, Ryerson RTA, Ryerson ProCom, Student Life Network, Yconic, Ideas Into Action, Resilient 100, and 55 Rush. You all helped me reinvent myself as a leader.

Much love to my partner, Bailey Parnell, as well as to my parents, to NBP, to Fyah, and to the Leals, Parnells, and Voigtlanders. Thank you all for your endless support and patience.

And special shout-out to the modern leaders who served as my muses for this book. Thank you to Bianca Marryshow, Chelsea Trimble, Anitta Krishnan, Kelsey Parnell, Faizan Mohammad, Tesni Ellis, Zakir Hemraj, Divyan Selvadurai, Kohulen Mahan, Lawrence Eta, James Hunt, Niki Strachan, Sally Anderson, Xolela Madlanga, and Steph Santos. I hope this book serves you well.

Last but not least, I'd like to express my deepest gratitude to Joe Cho, Samantha Holland, and the entire team at Callisto Media. Thank you all for the opportunity to not only write this book, but to be written by it.

ABOUT THE AUTHOR

Hamza Khan is a multi-award-winning marketer, best-selling author of *The Burnout Gamble*, and global keynote speaker whose TEDx talk "Stop Managing, Start Leading" has been viewed over a million times. He is a top-ranked university educator, serial entrepreneur, and respected thought leader whose insights have been featured by notable media outlets such as *Vice*, *Business Insider*, and *The Globe and Mail*. He empowers youth and early talent through his work as managing director of Student Life Network, Canada's largest and most comprehensive education resource platform, which reaches over 2.7 million students. From TEDx stages and international conferences to MBA classrooms and *Fortune* 500 boardrooms, Hamza is invited regularly to deliver keynotes and workshops around the world. His clients have included companies and organizations like PepsiCo, LinkedIn, Deloitte, PwC, Trivago, and over 100 colleges and universities. Learn more at HamzaKhan.ca.